THIS BOAT COLORING BOOK BELONGS TO

Dear Parents!

This Coloring book will help to increase the drawing skill & the color sense of your child.

This Coloring Book will help Your to be more Active, Attentive and Focused to learn New Things.

My hope is that Your Little One Loves this Book and Enjoys every single page. If they do, Please think about Giving us your honest feedback via a review on Amazon. It may take only a moment, but it really does mean the world for small business like us.

The mission of KIDDO EDU ZONE is to create Premium contents for children that will help them learn new things, grow their imaginations, improve their skill and have lots of fun along the way.

This Boat Coloring Book has been created with much love & care.

Without You, However, this would not be possible. So We sincerely thank you for your purchase and for supporting our mission.

Support us on KIDDO EDU ZONE.

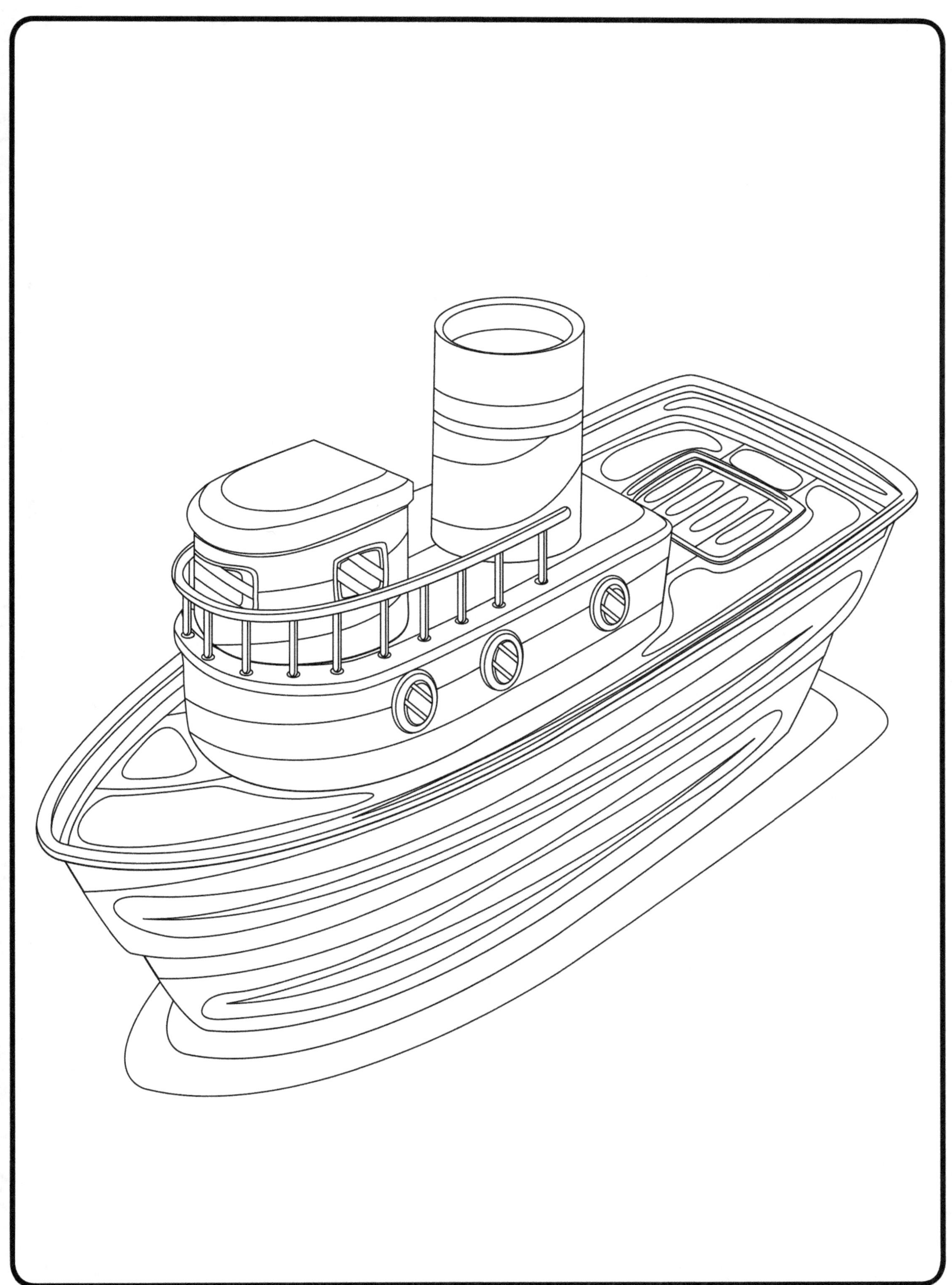

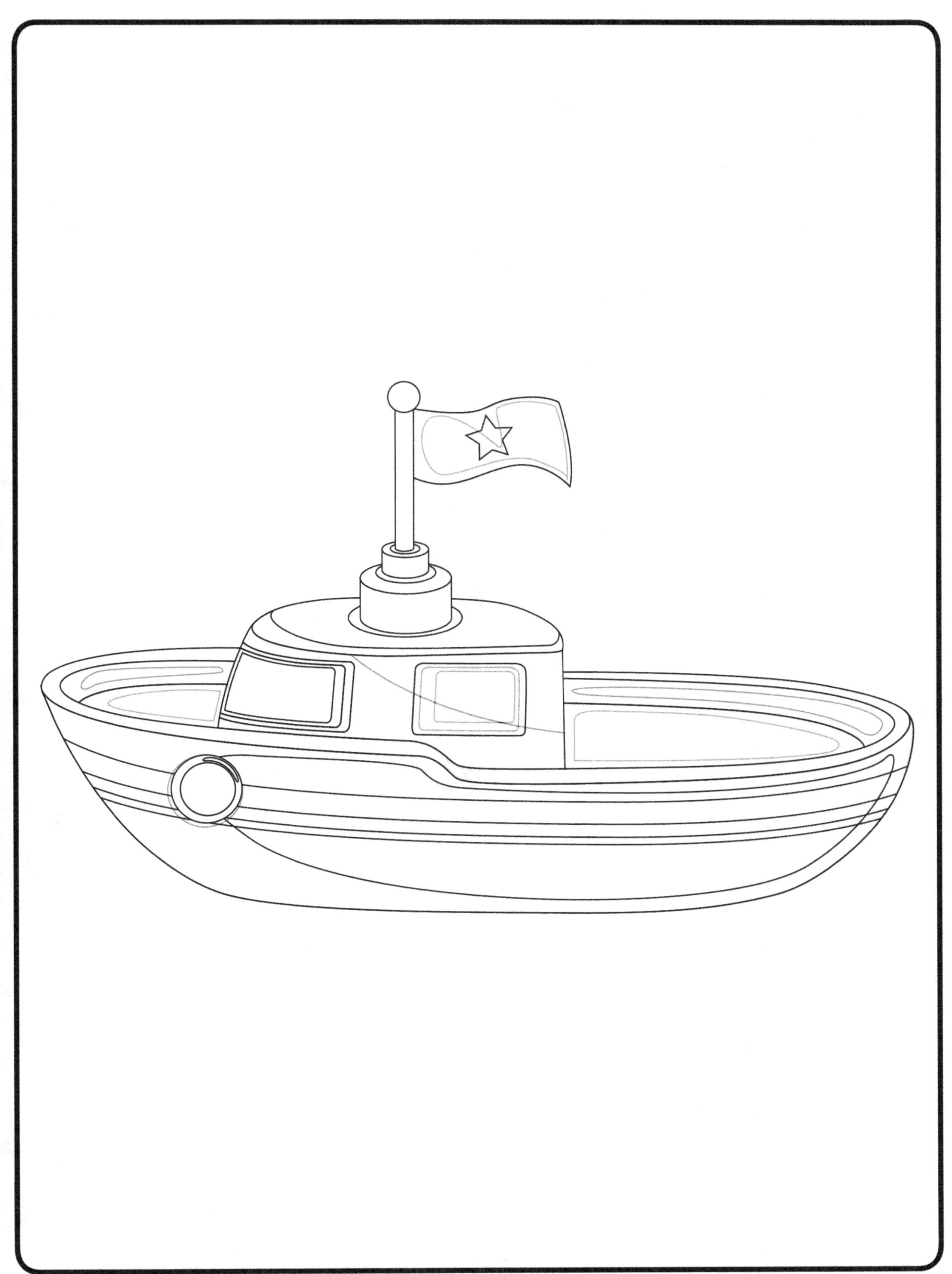

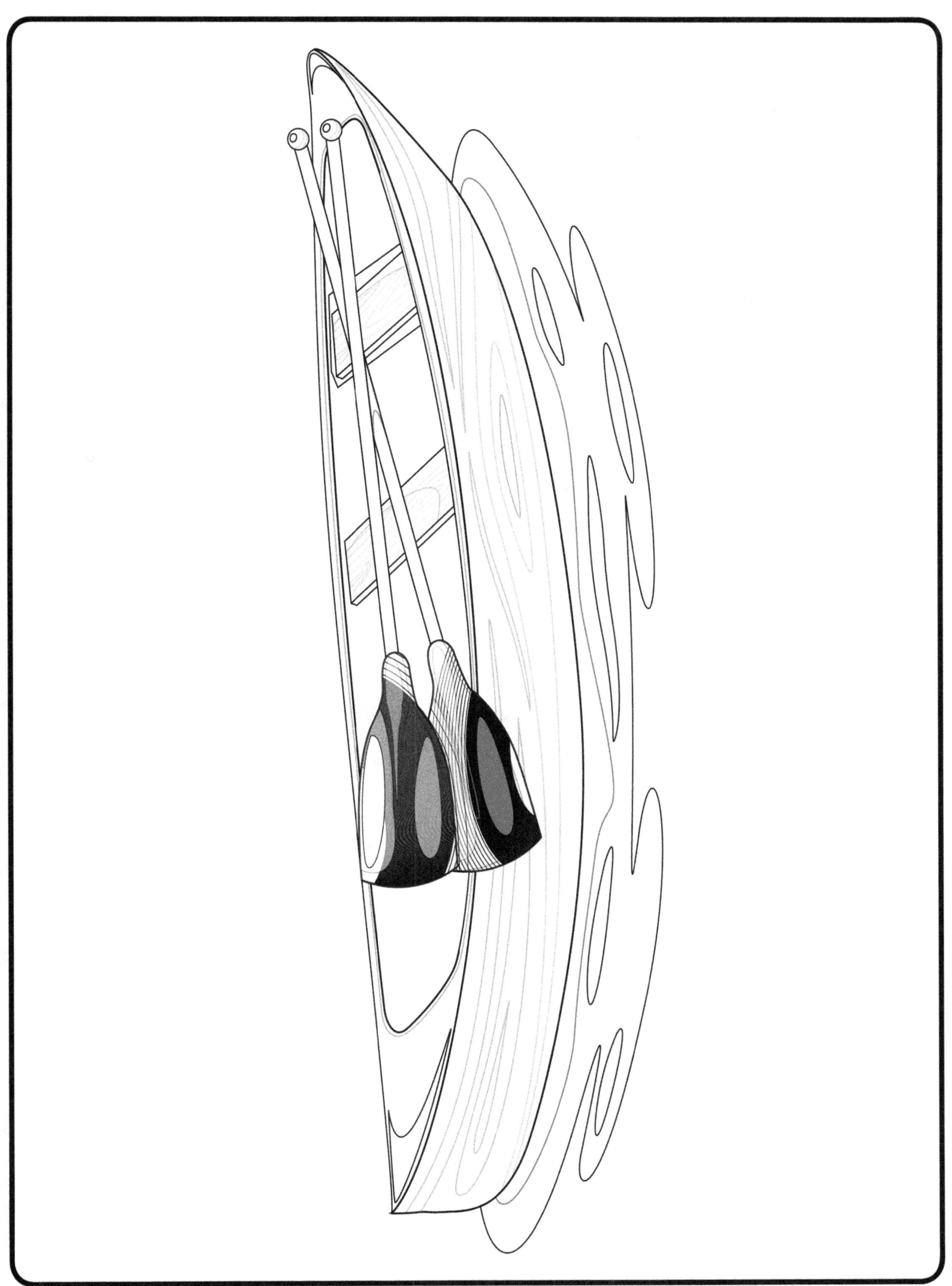

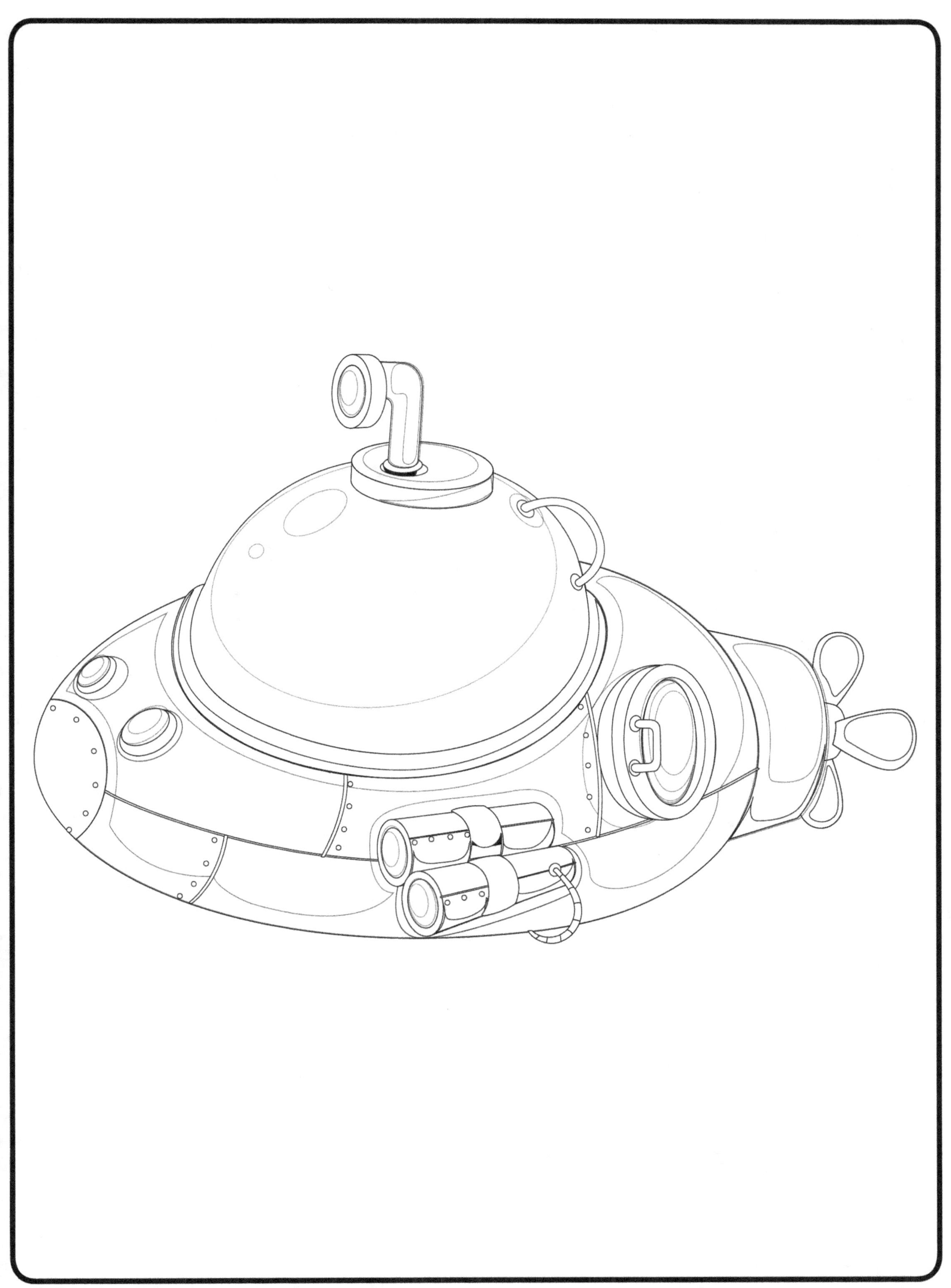

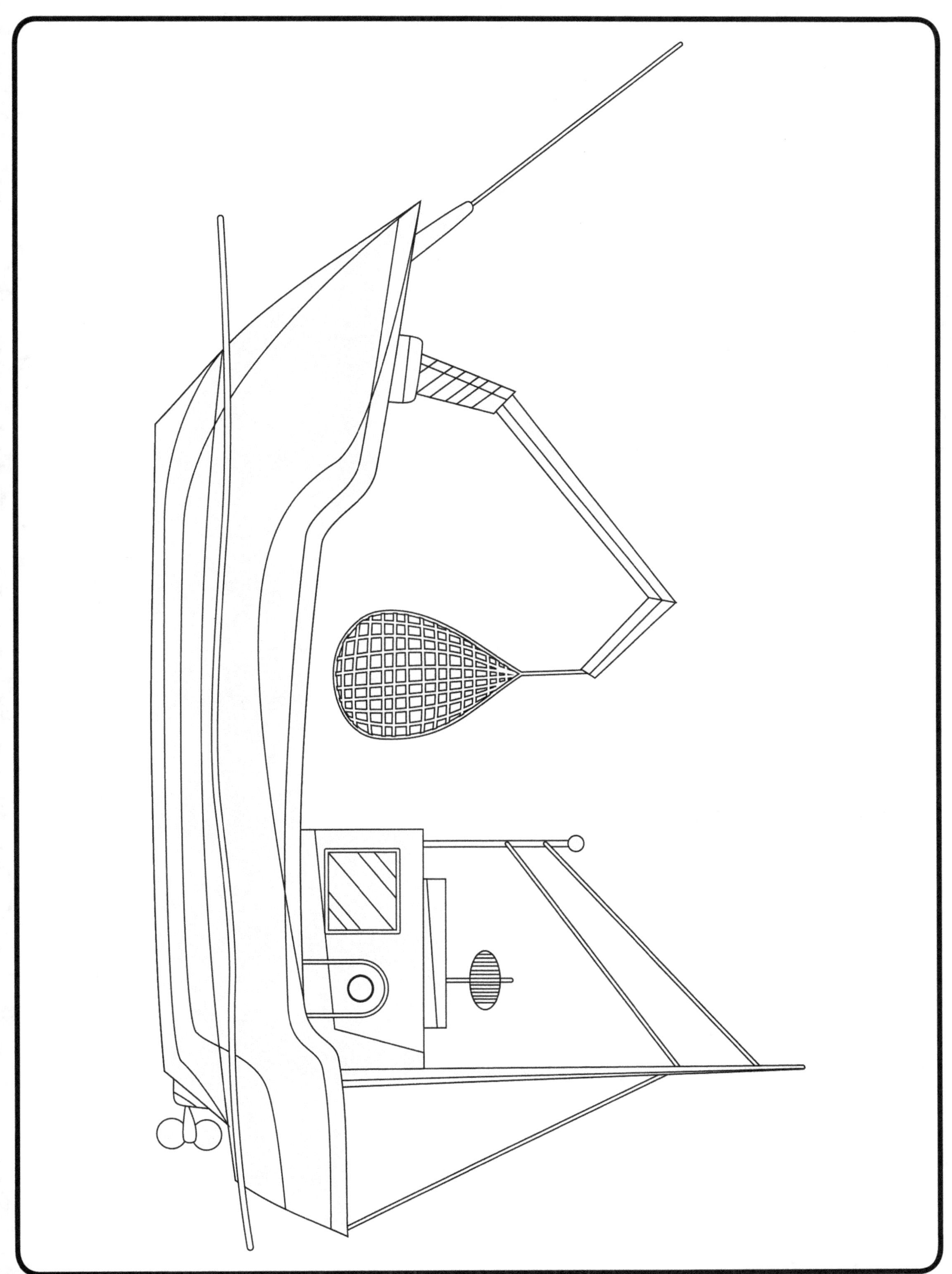

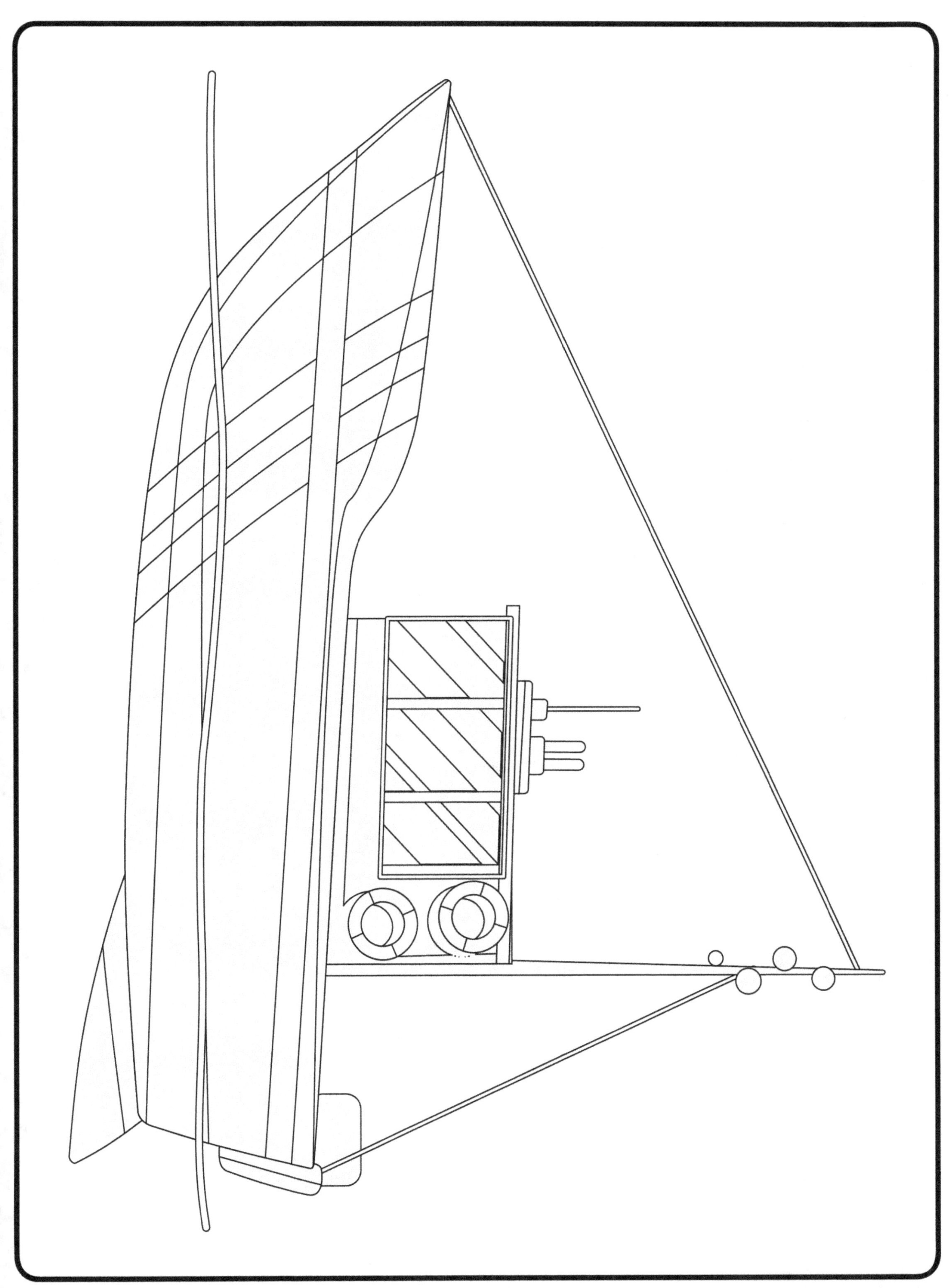

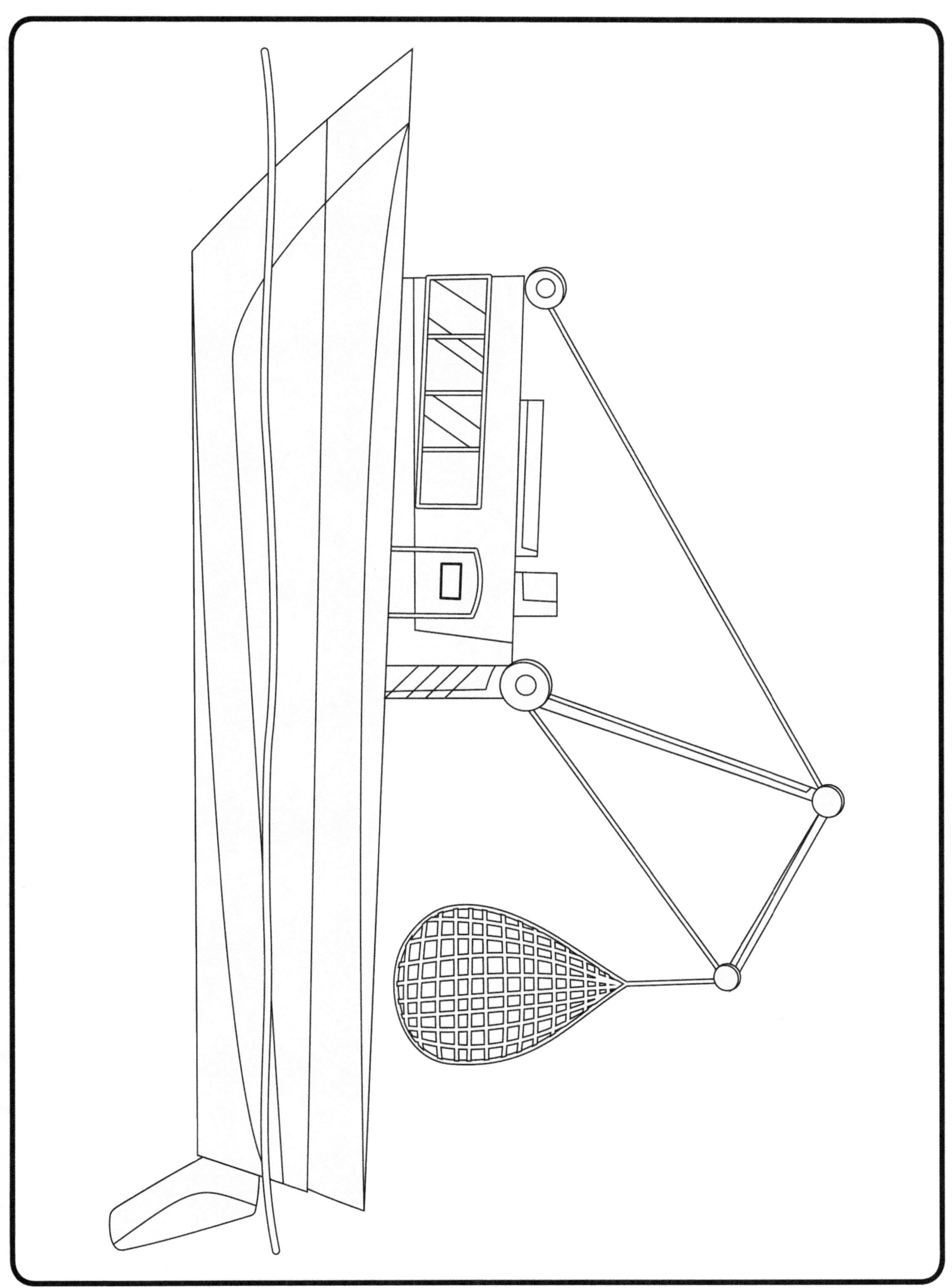

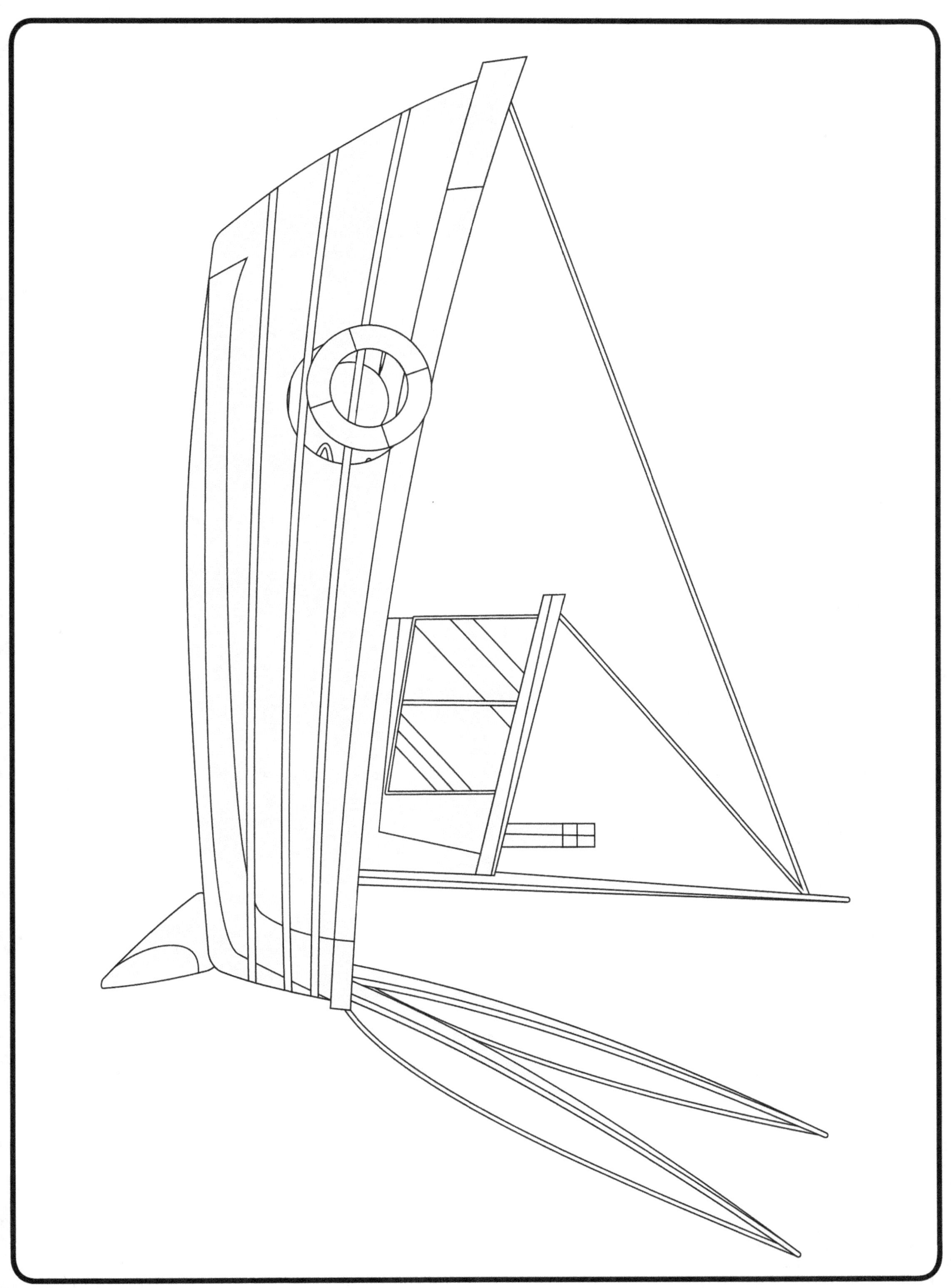

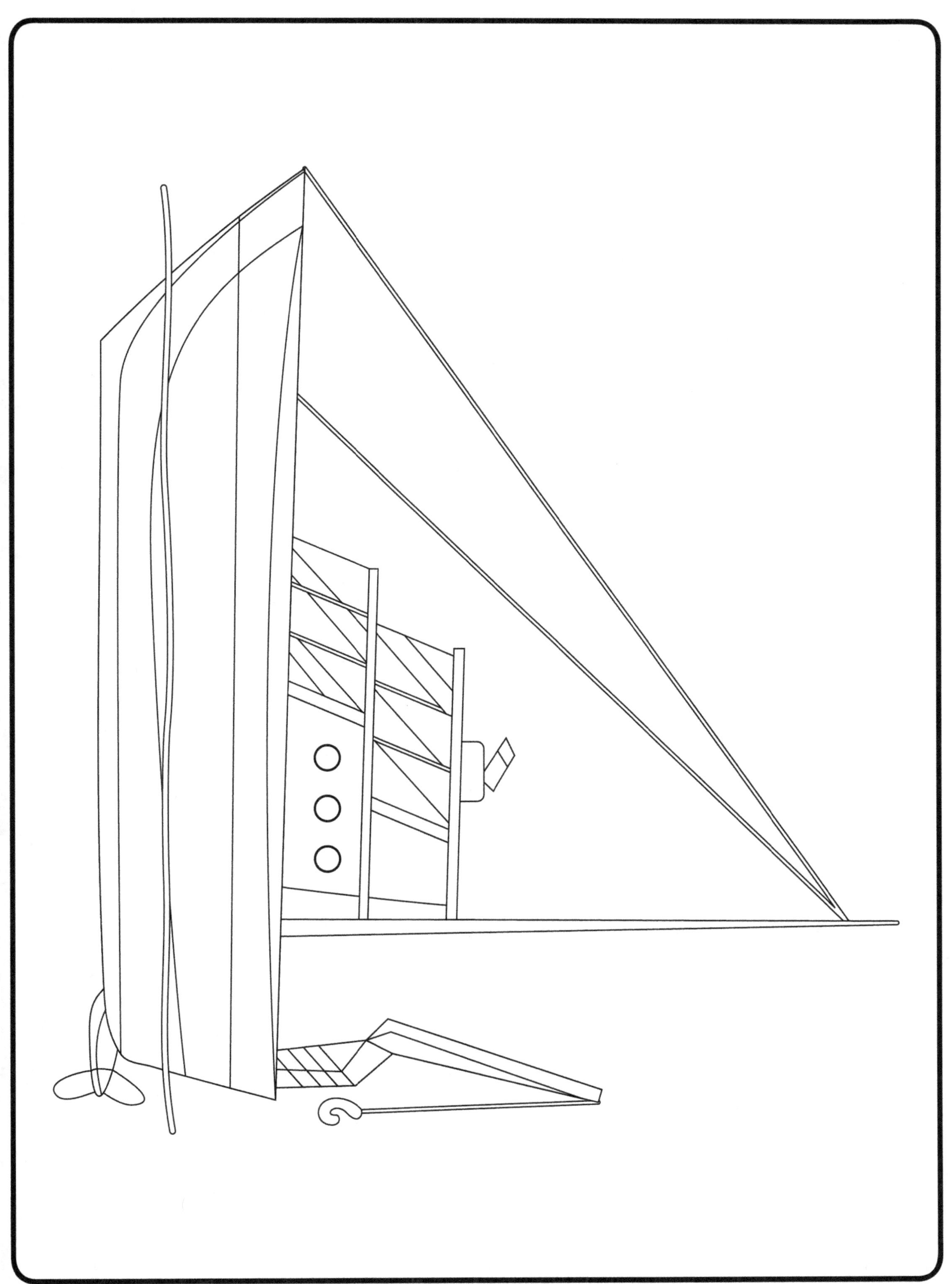

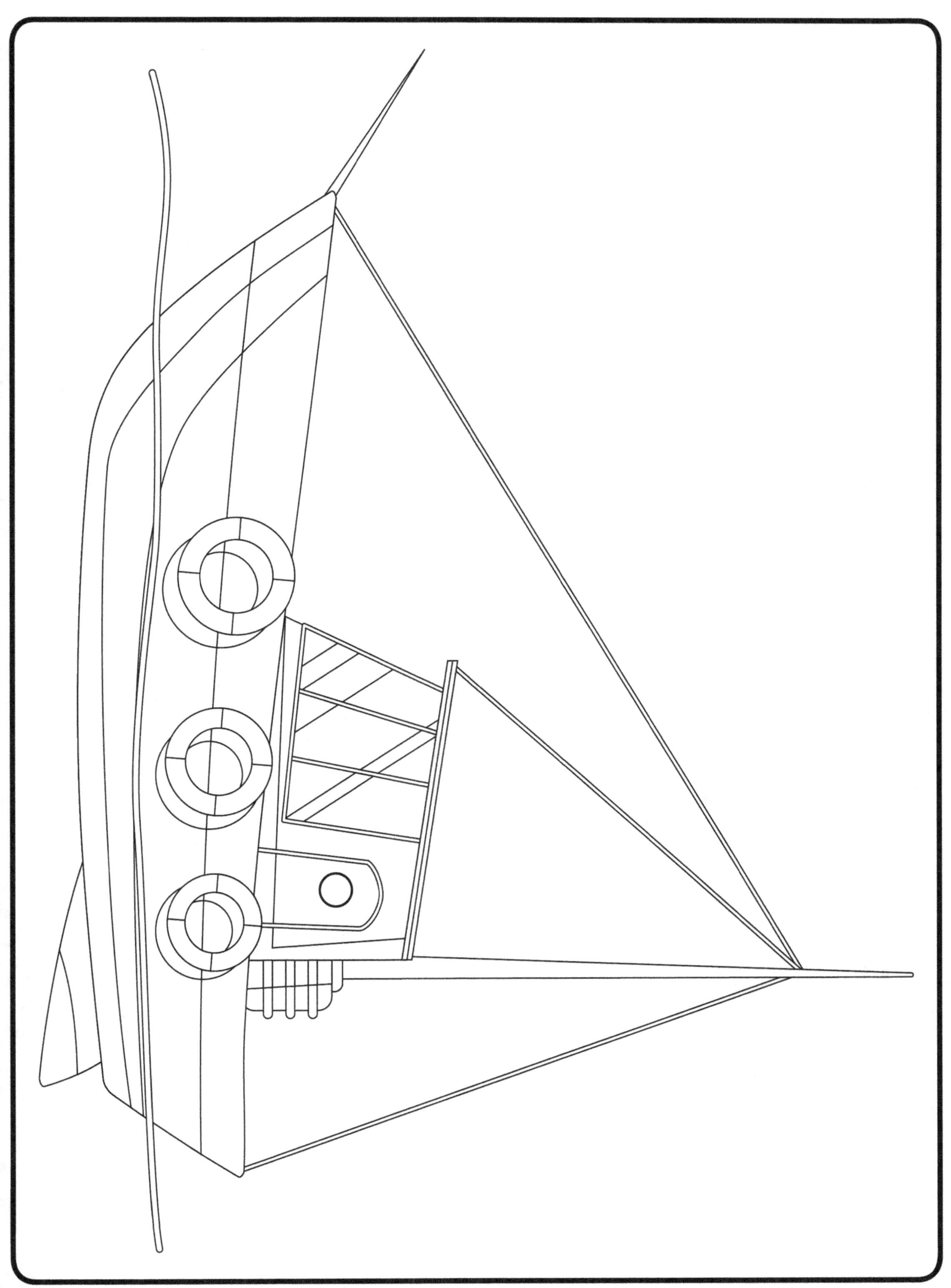

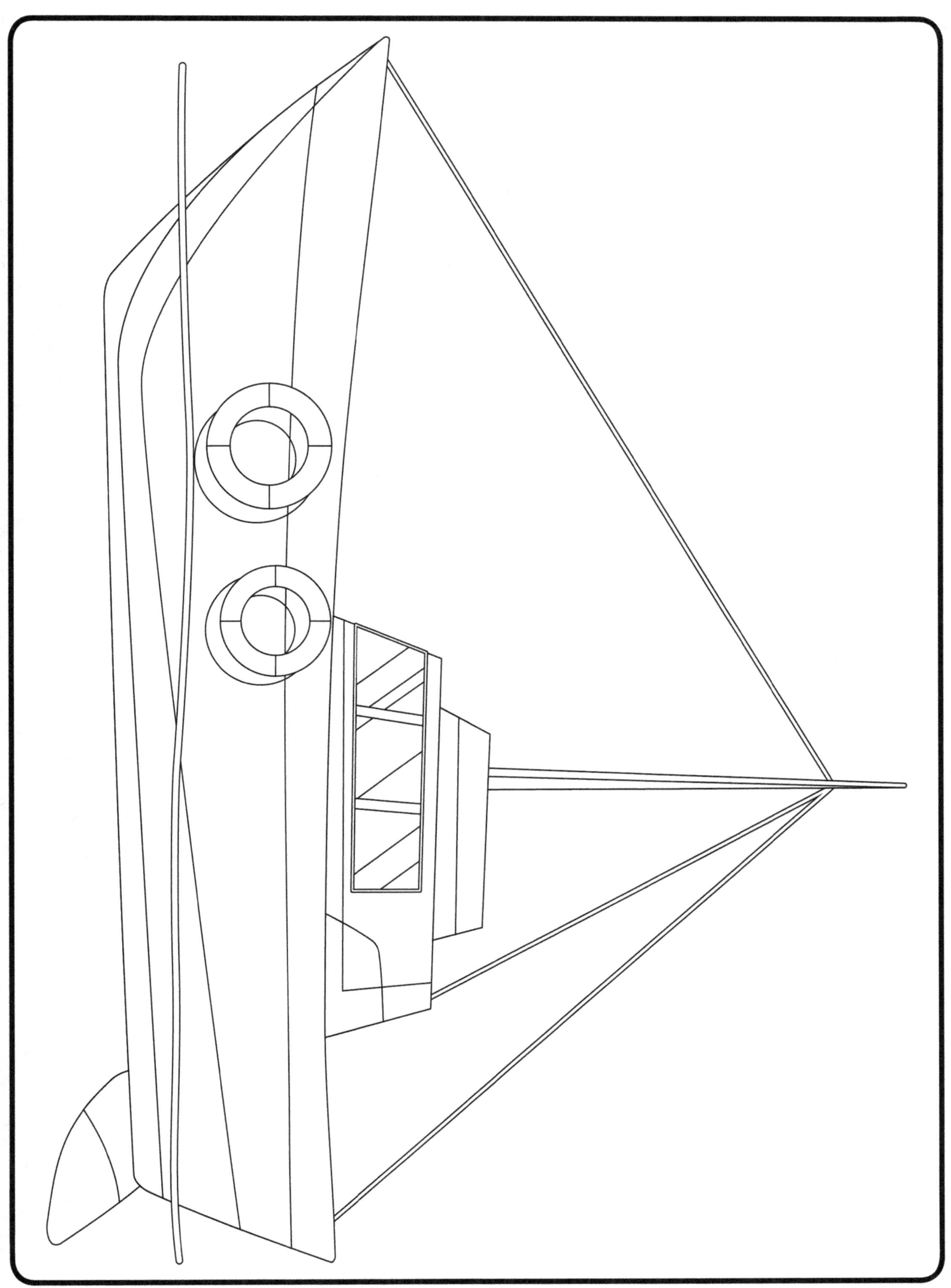

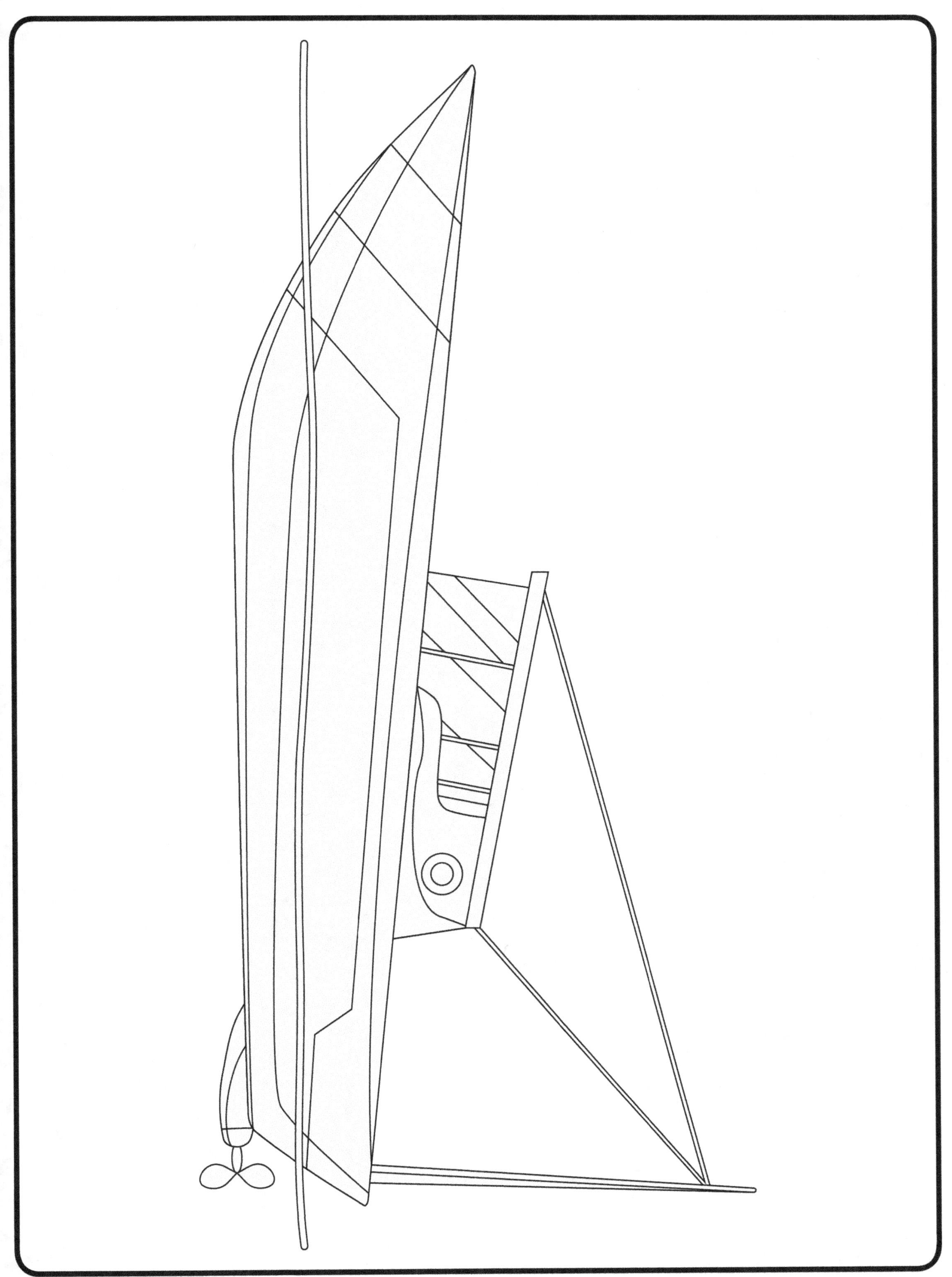

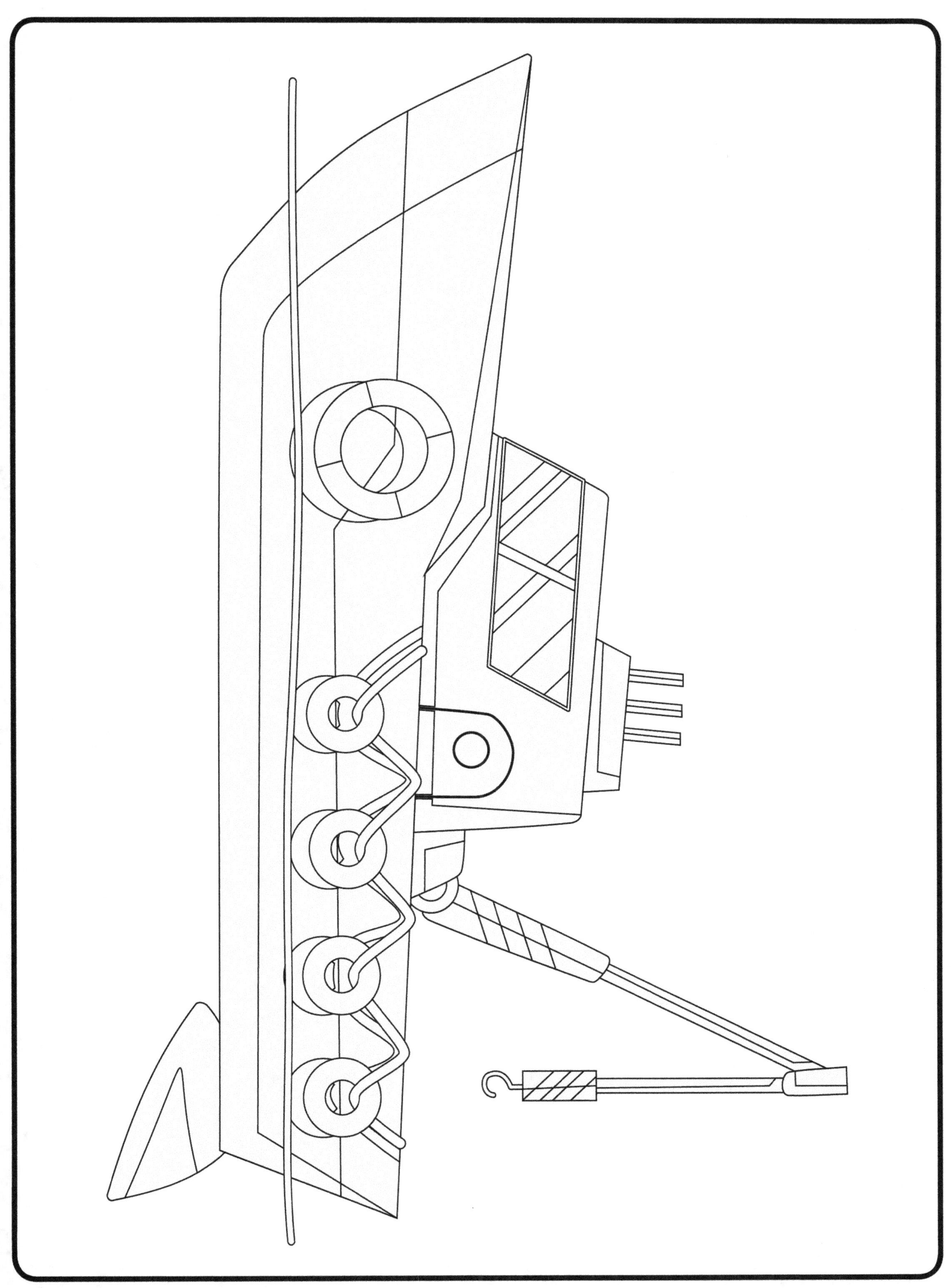

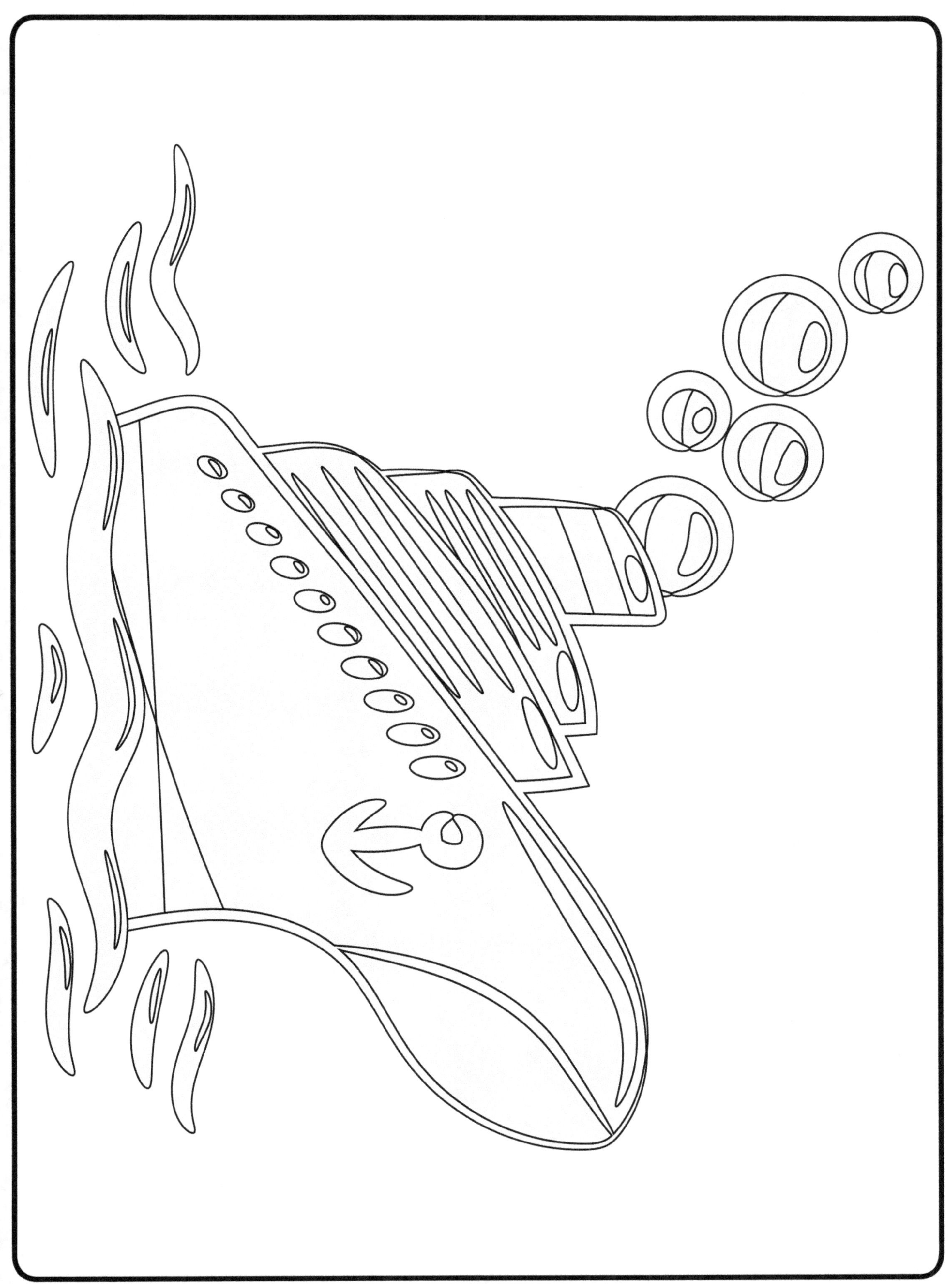

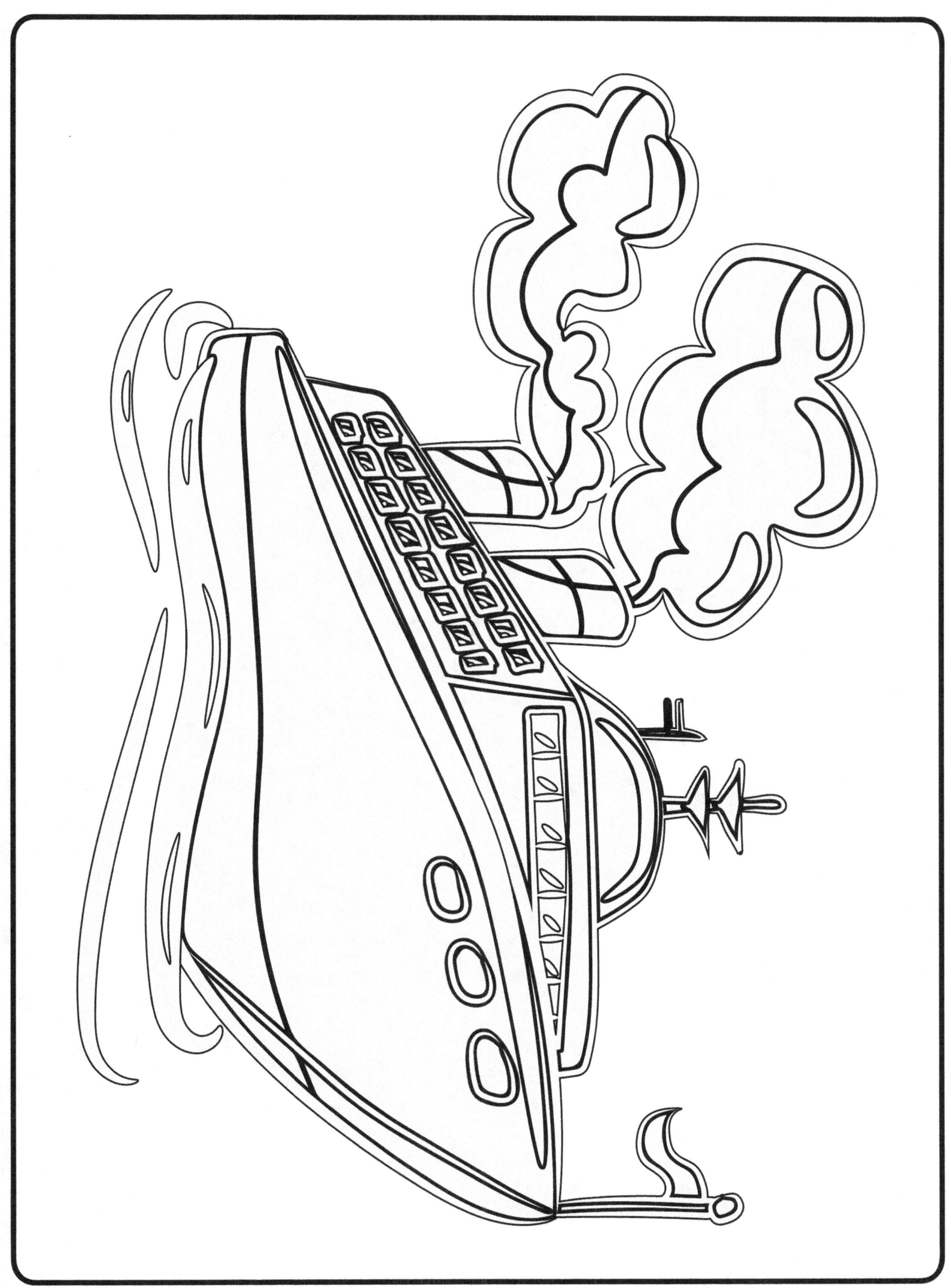

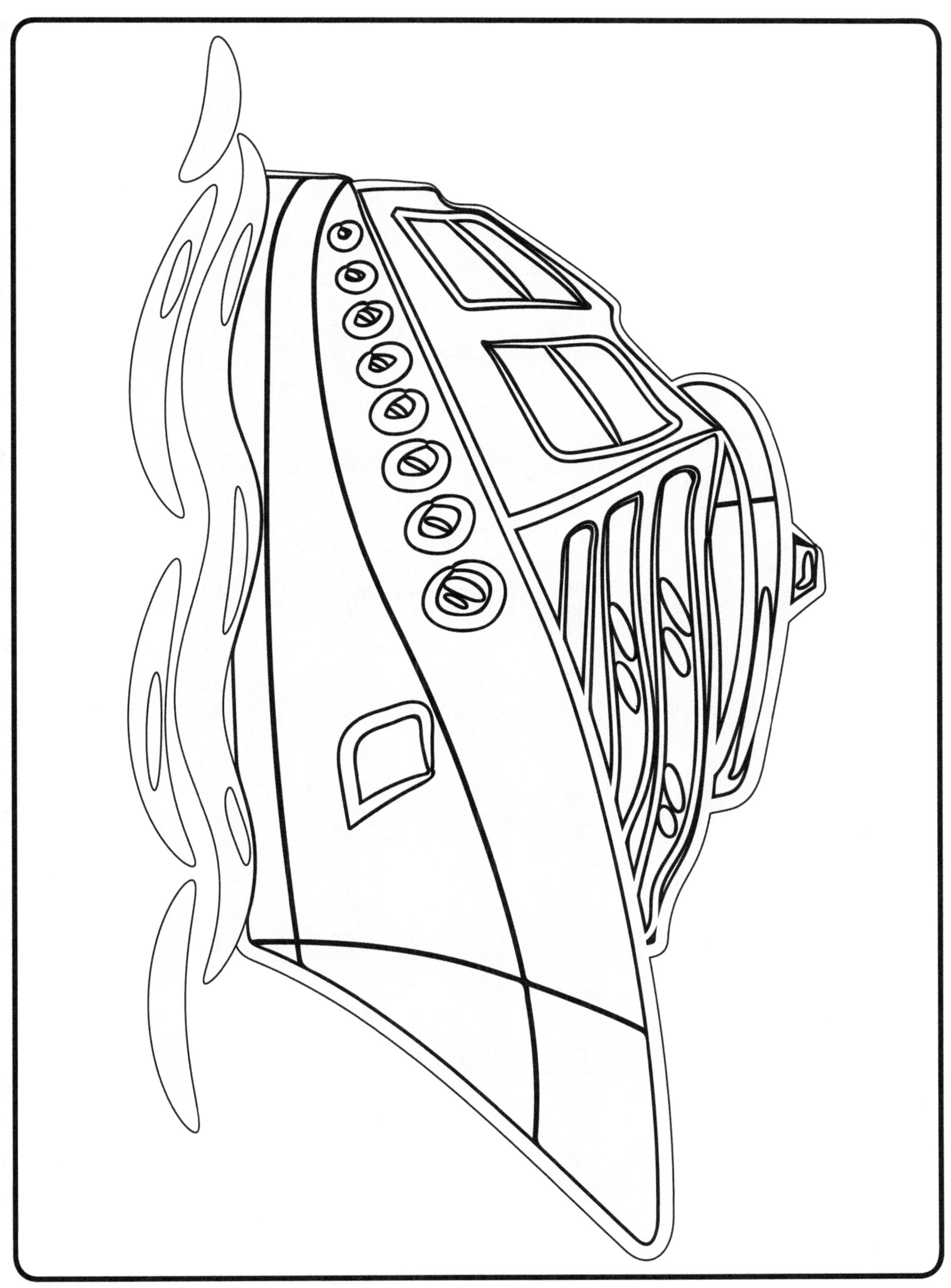

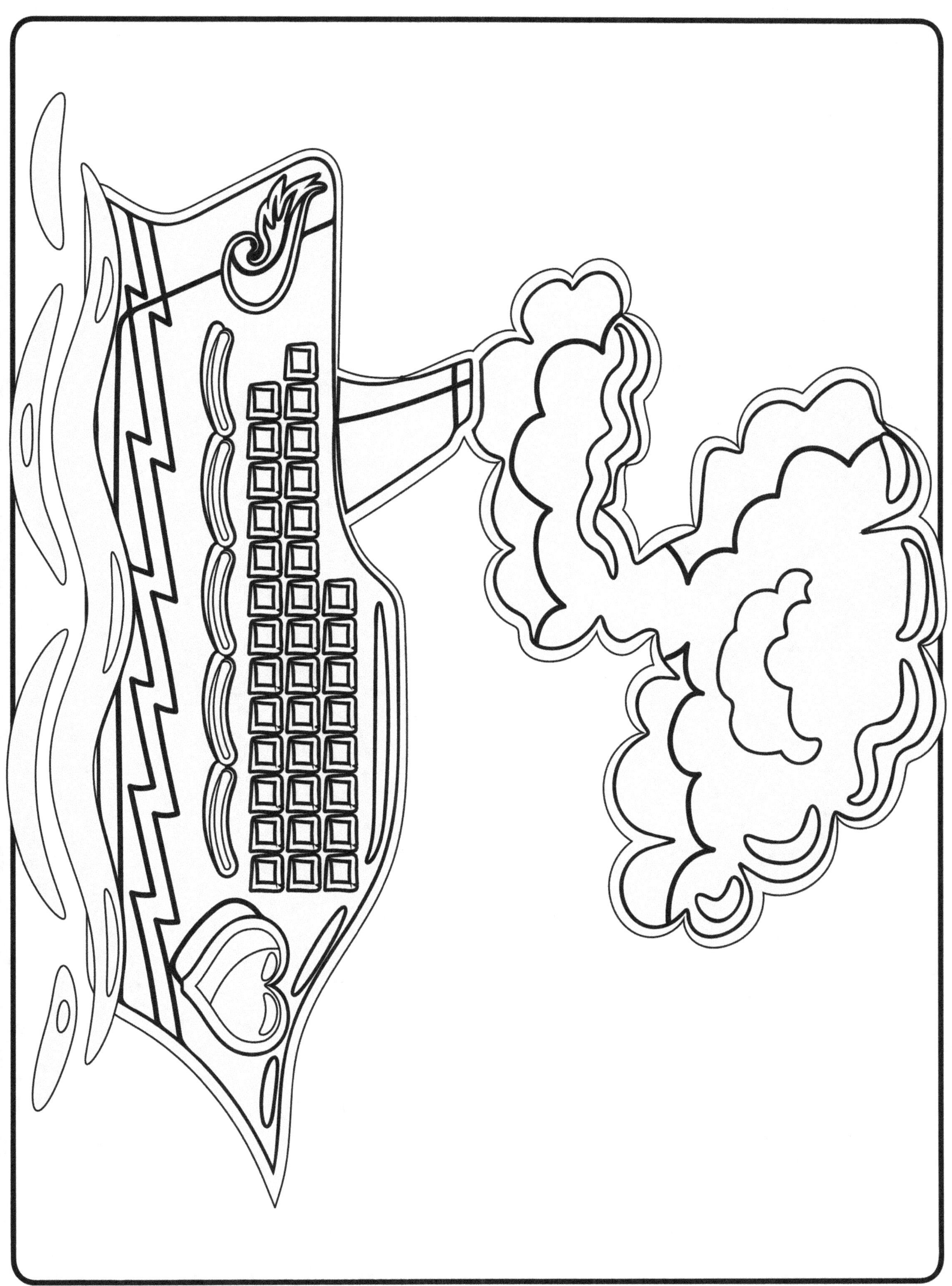

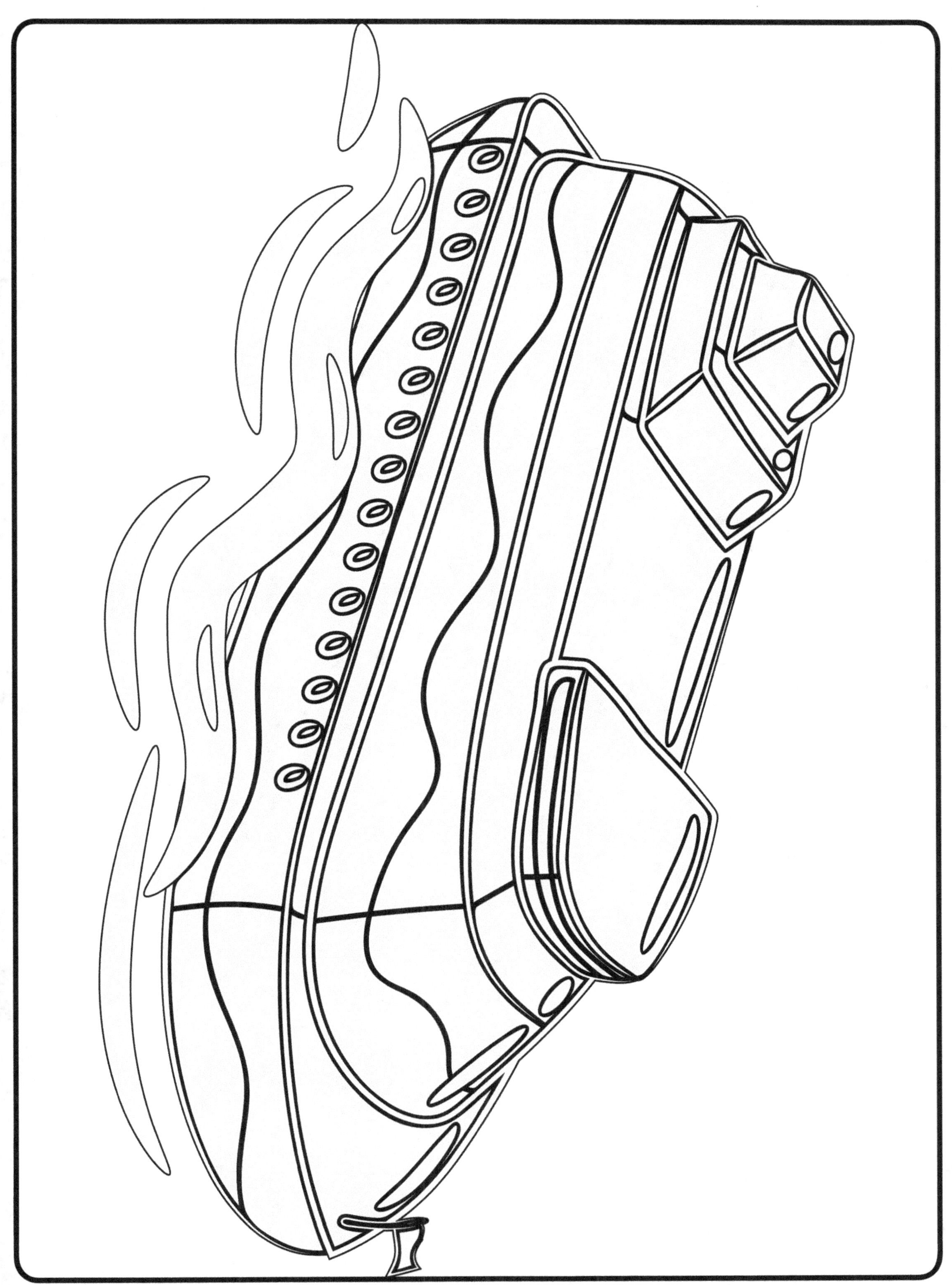

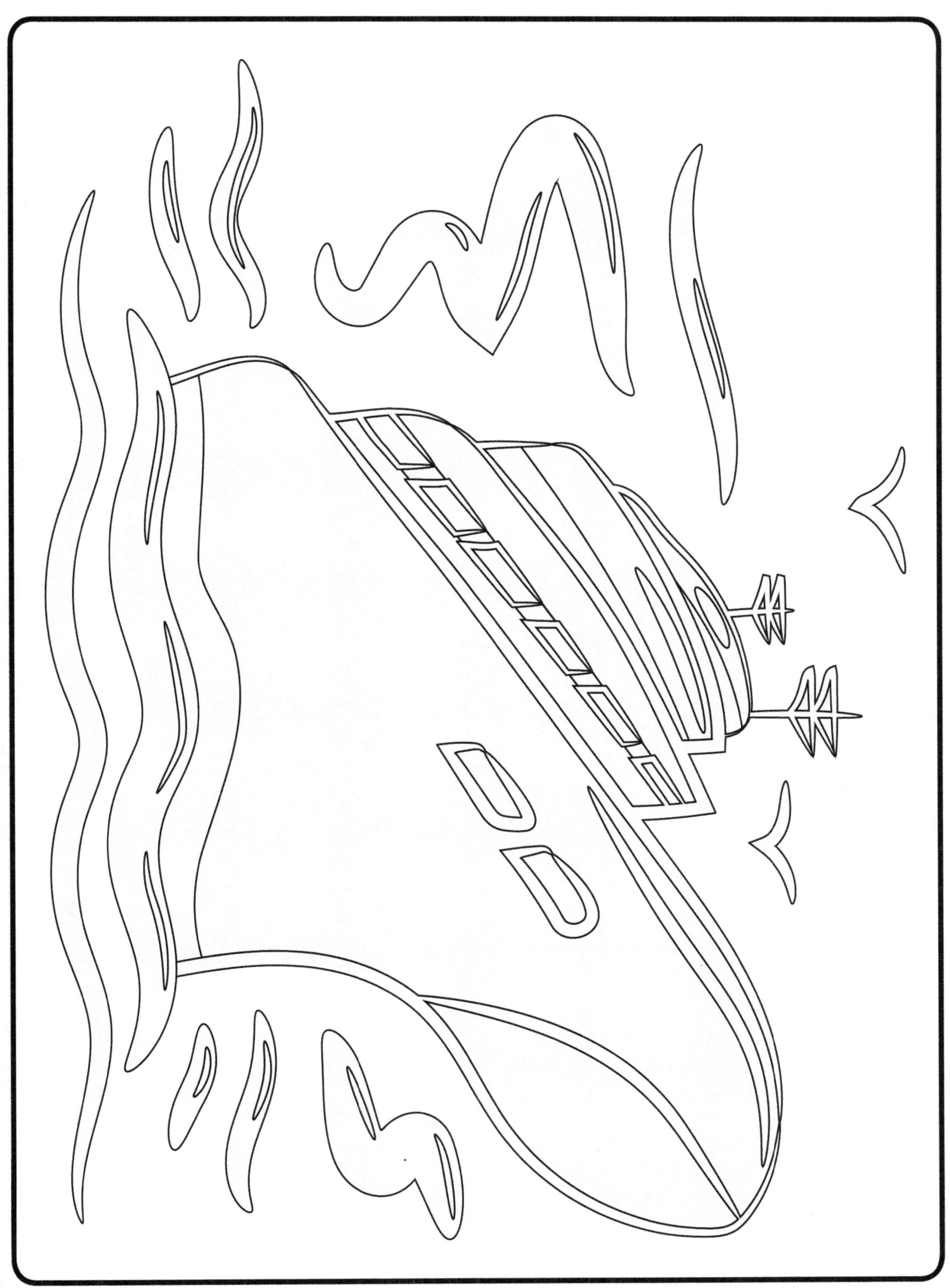

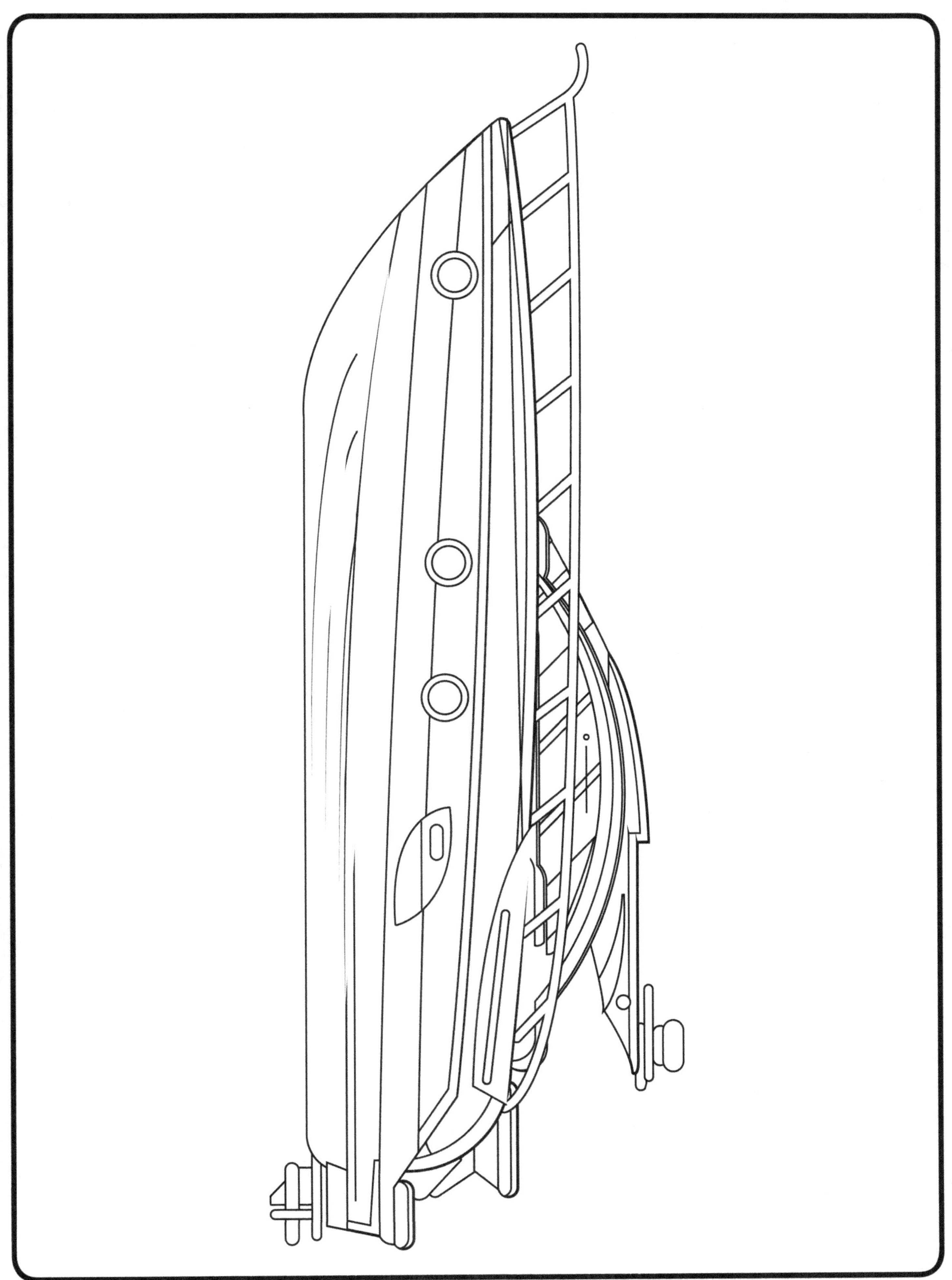

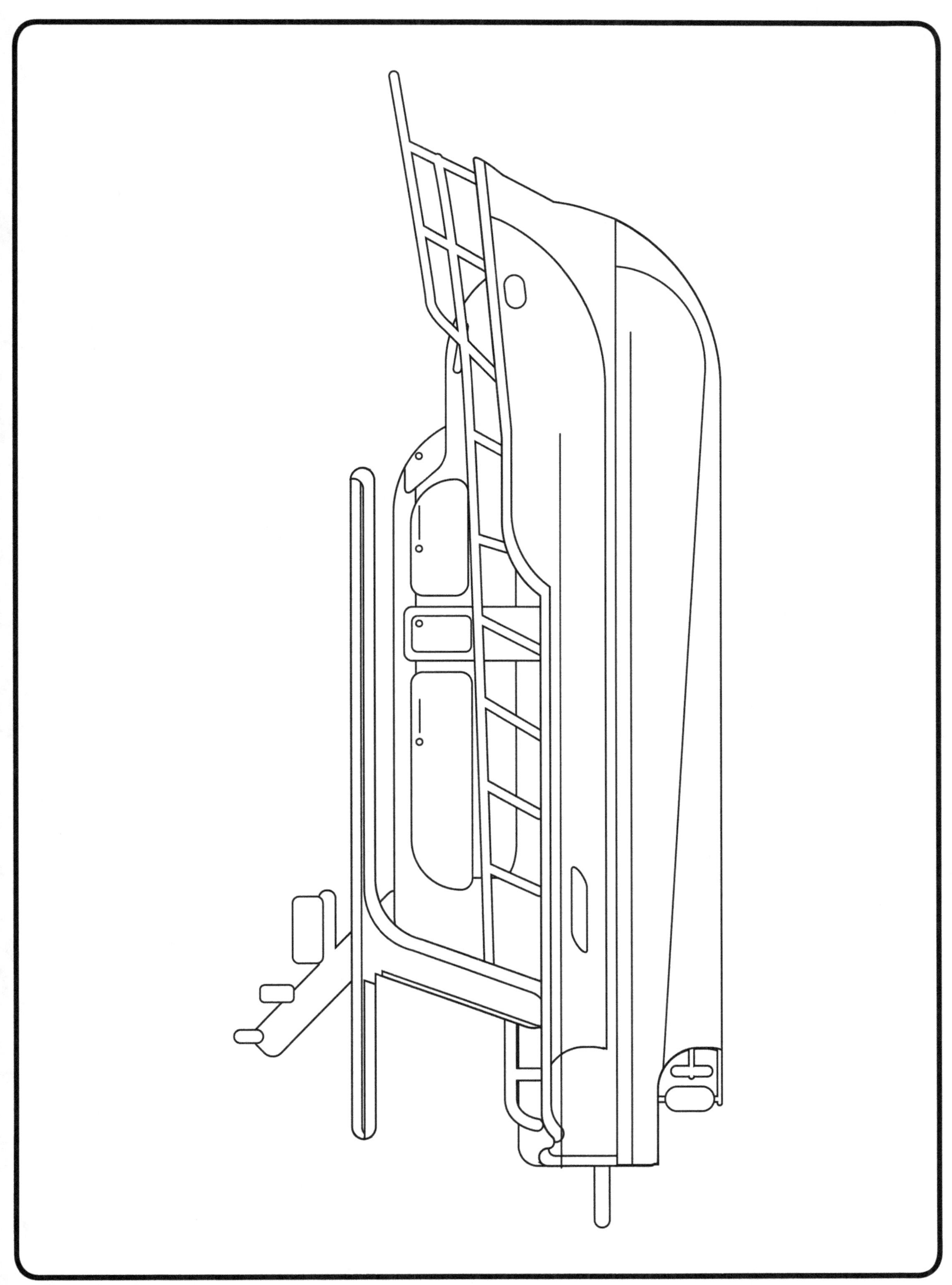

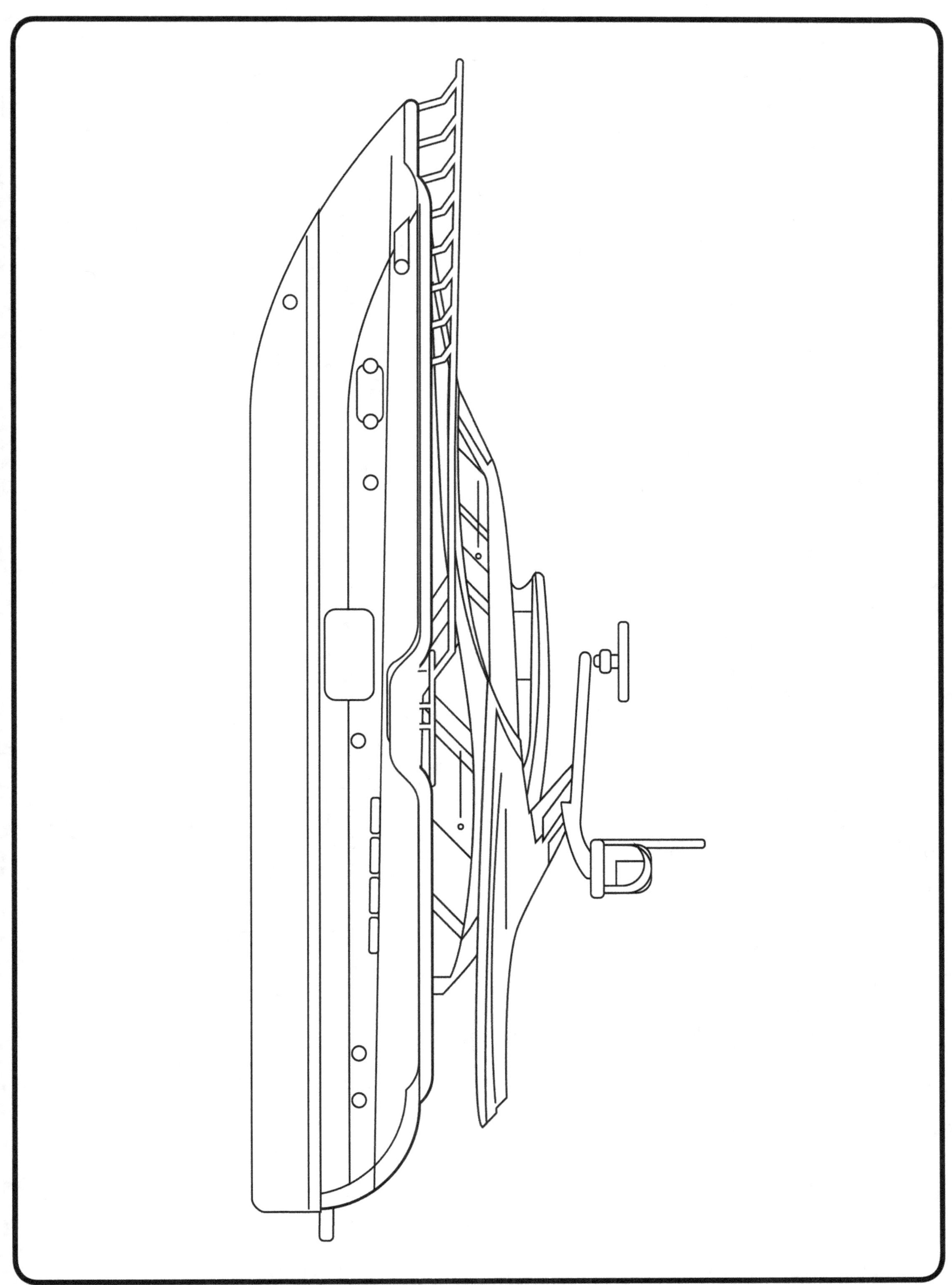

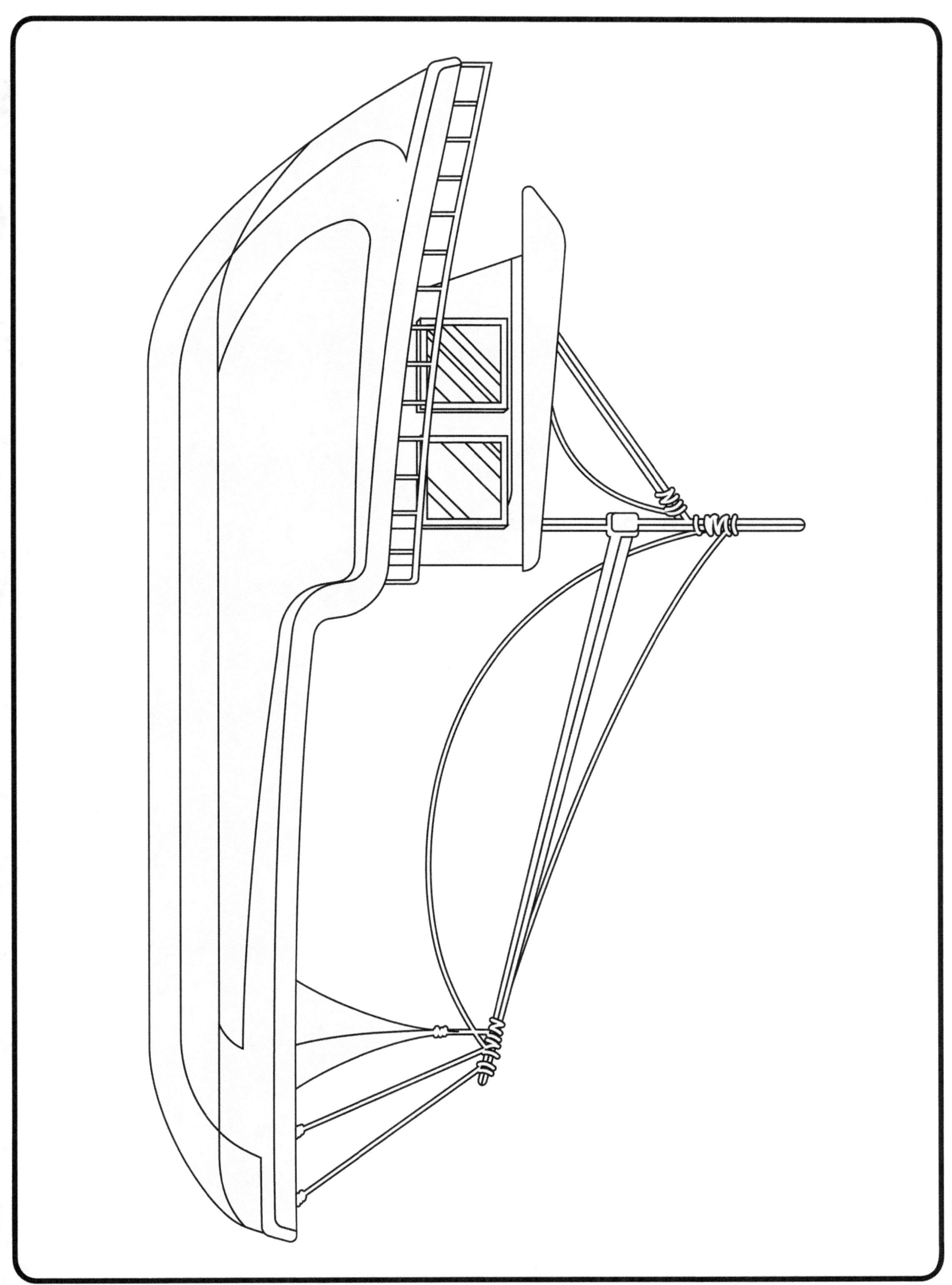

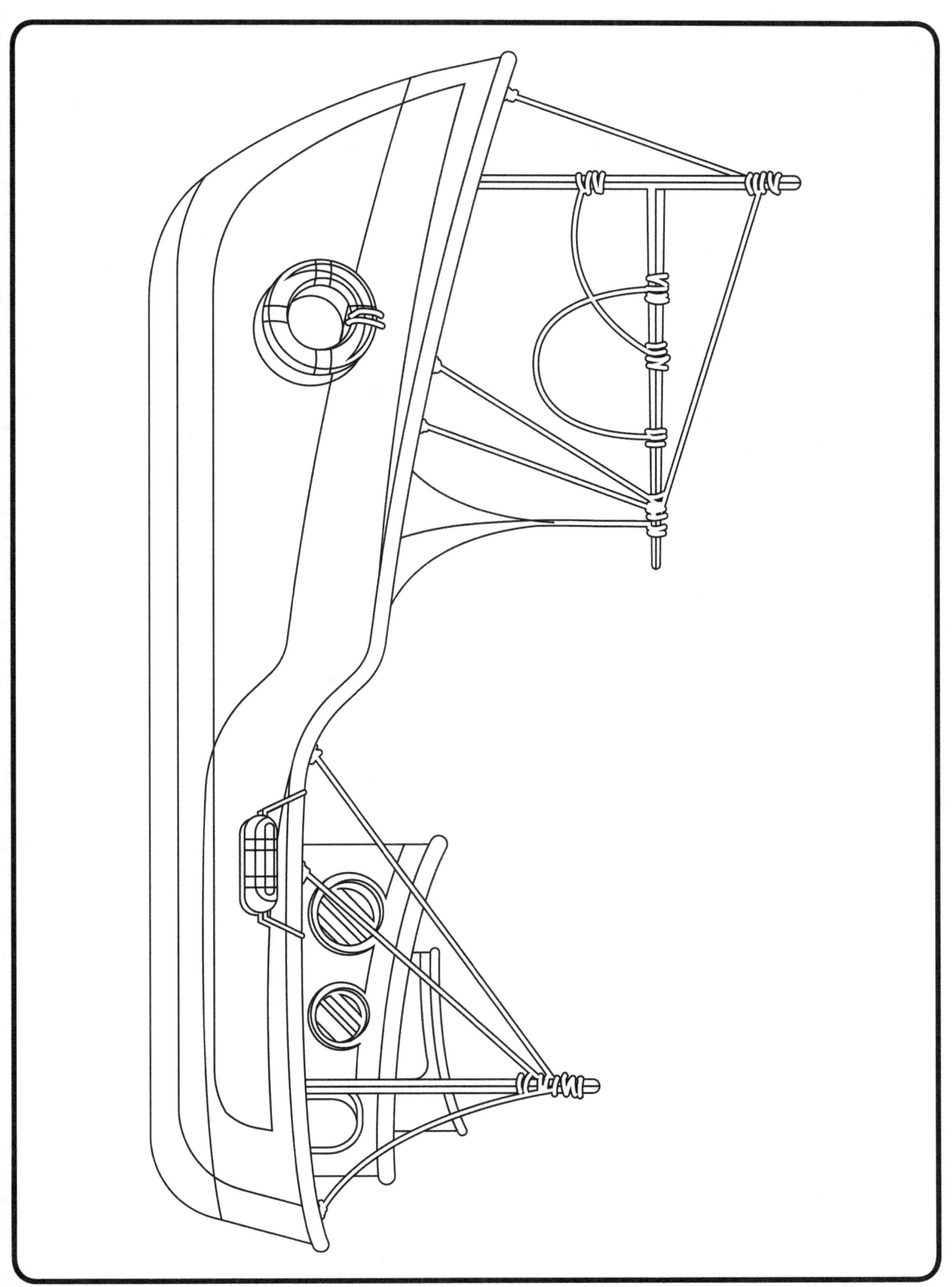

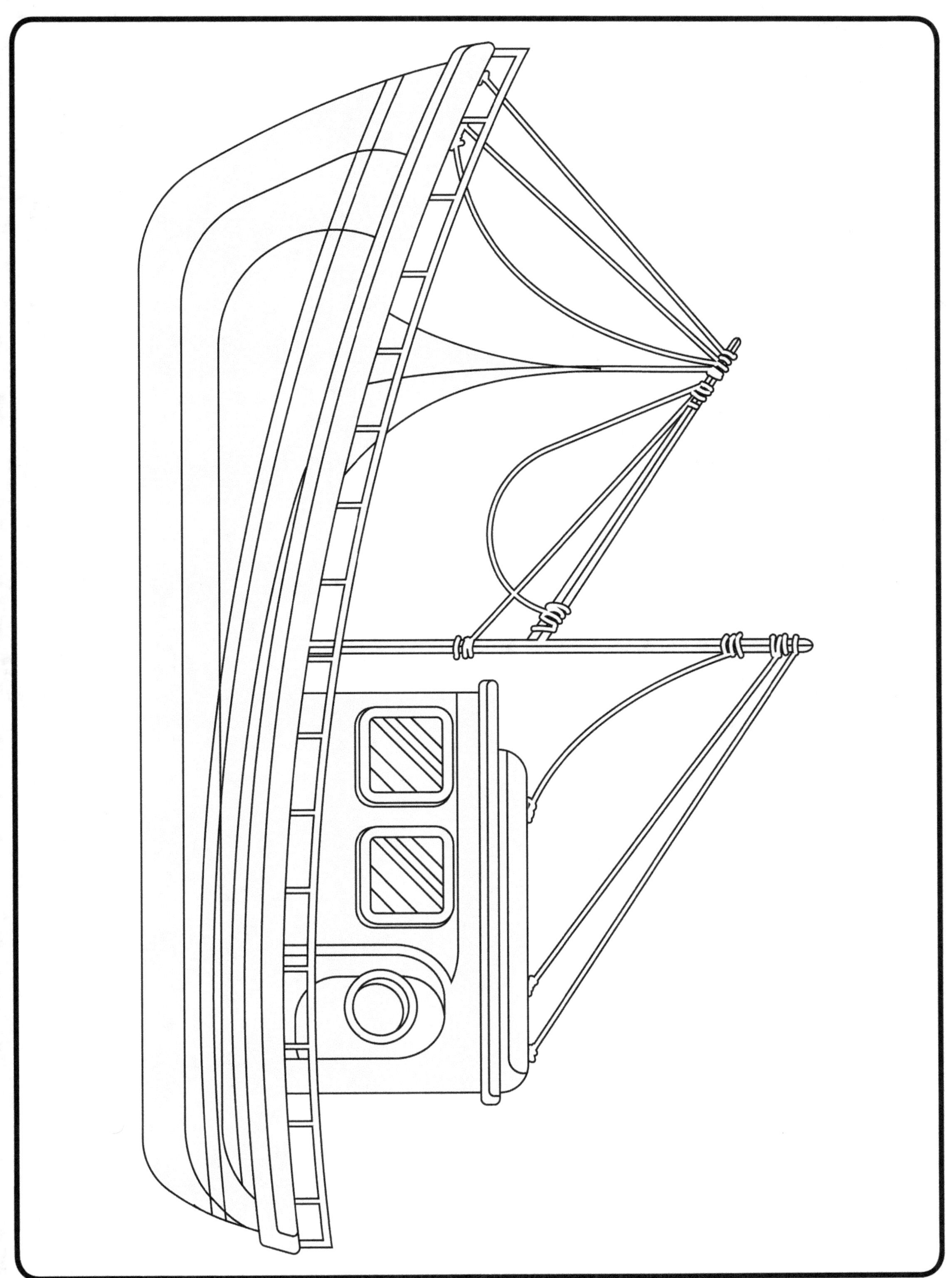

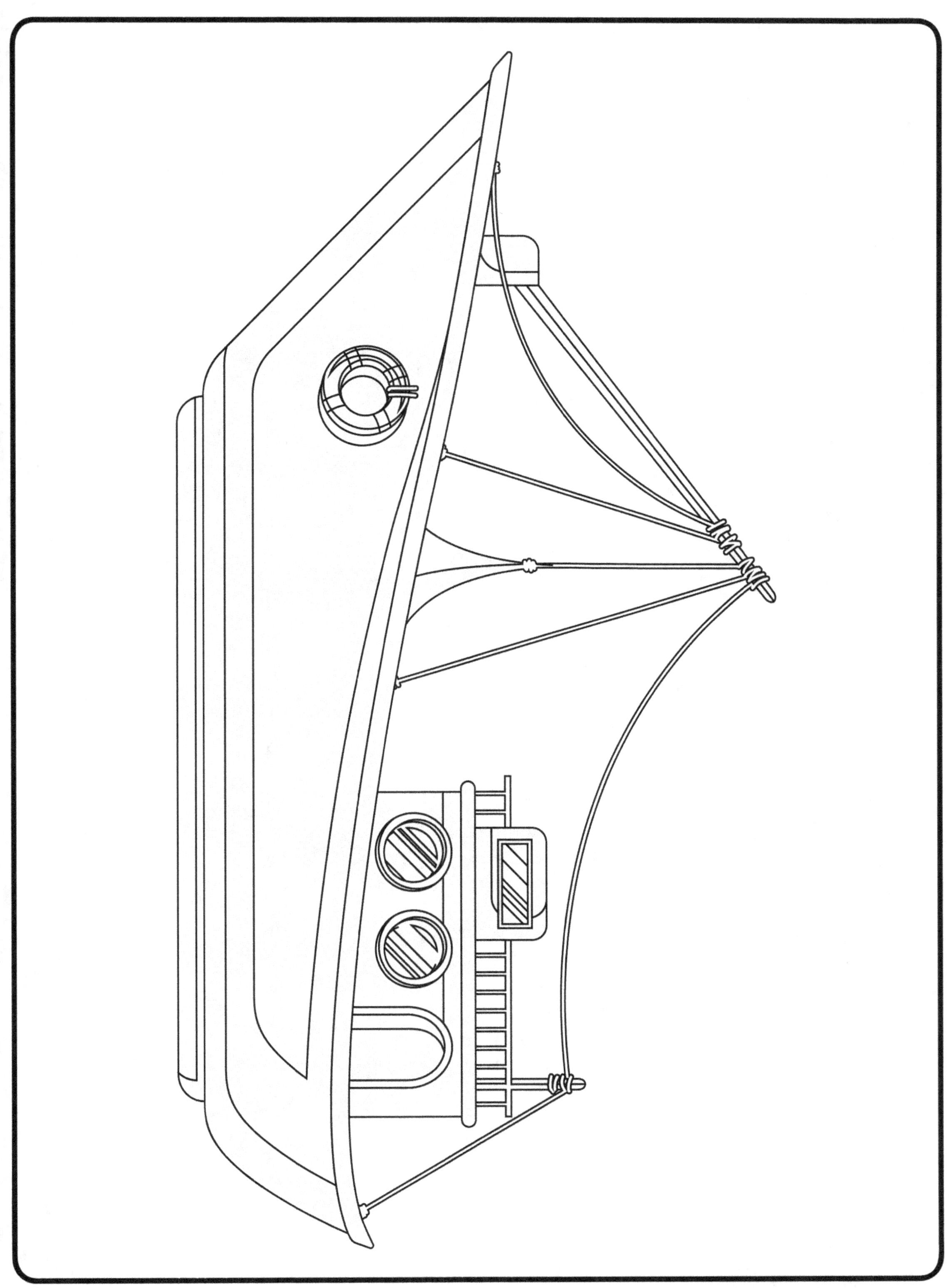

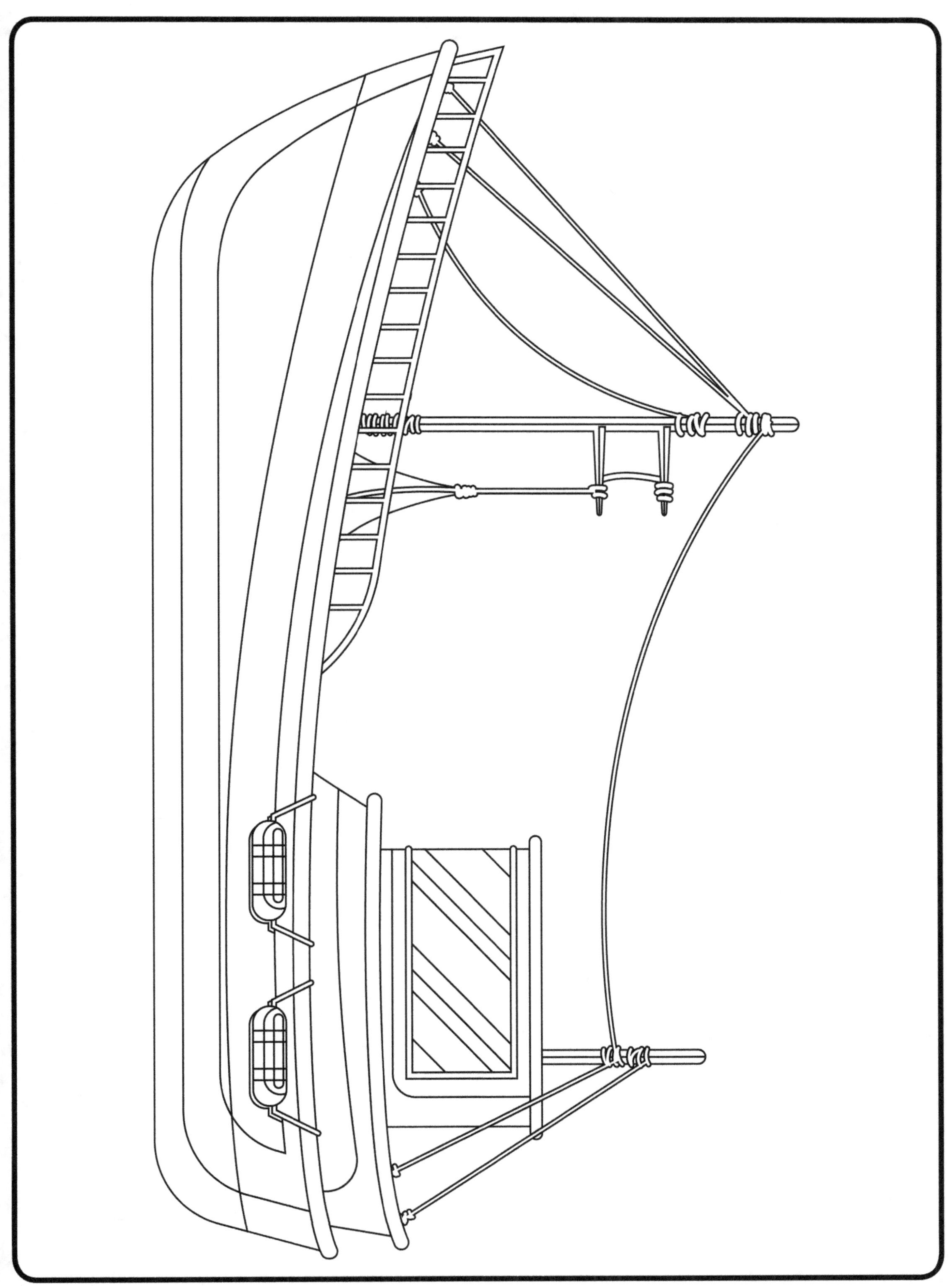

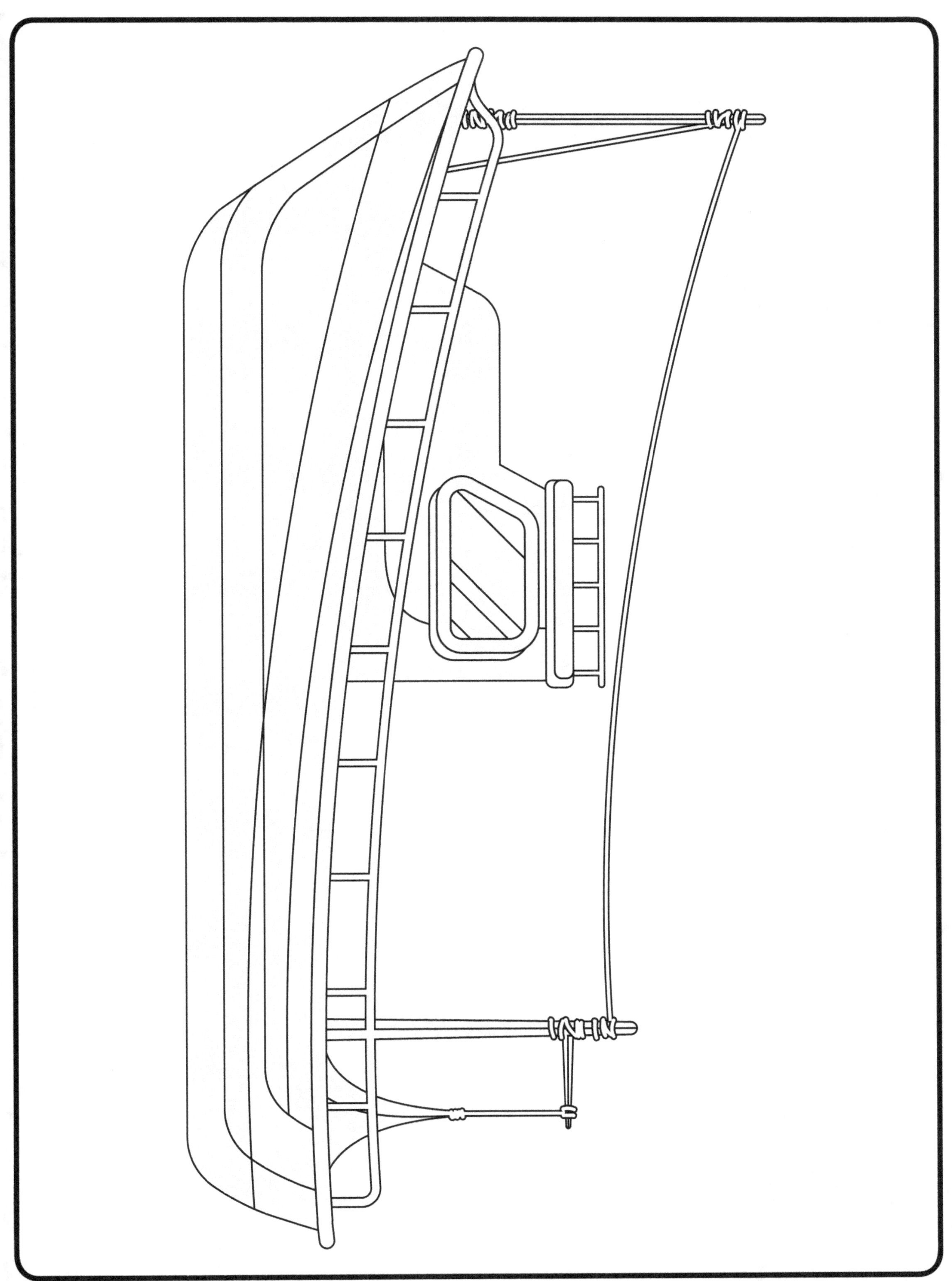

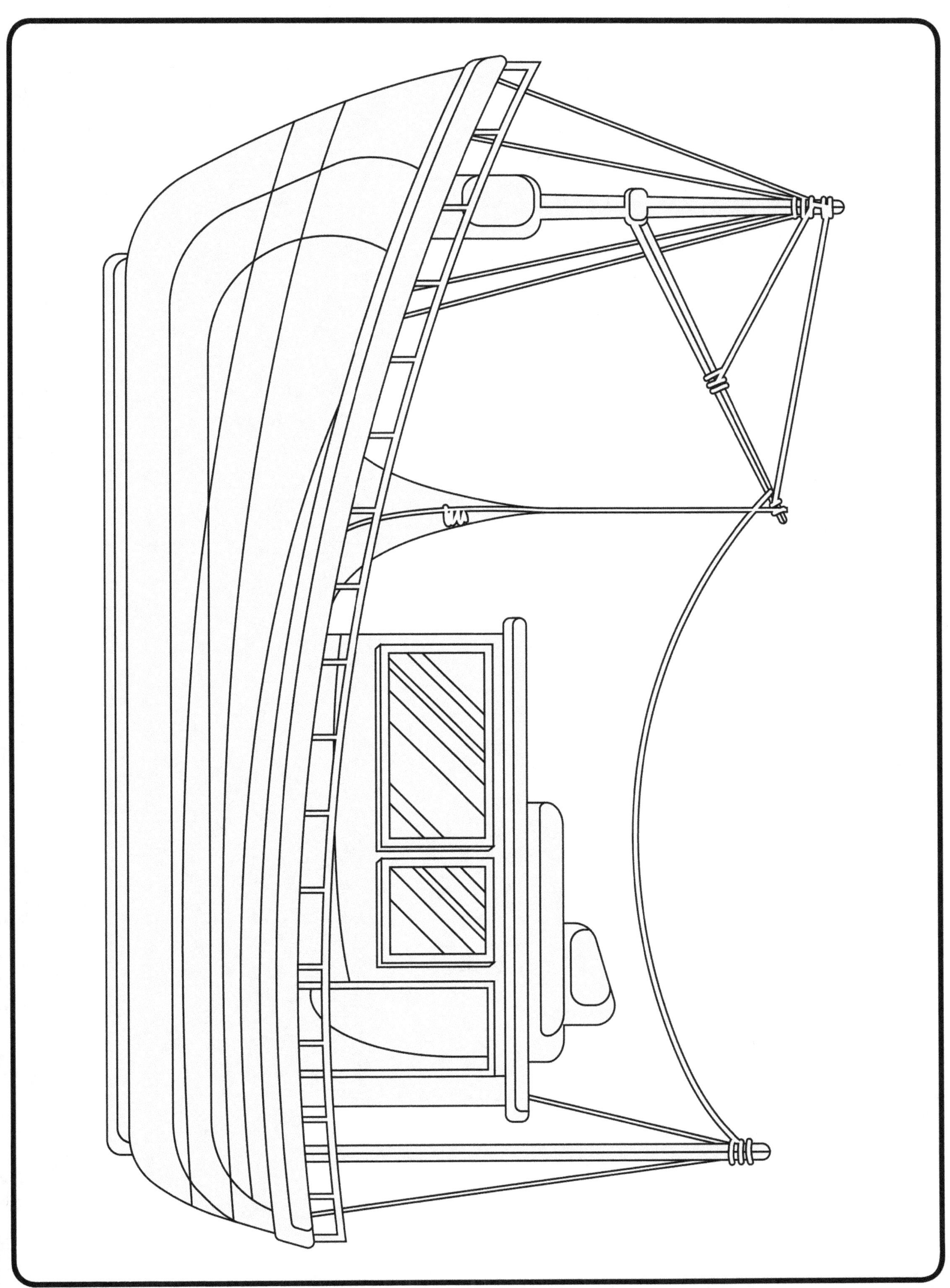

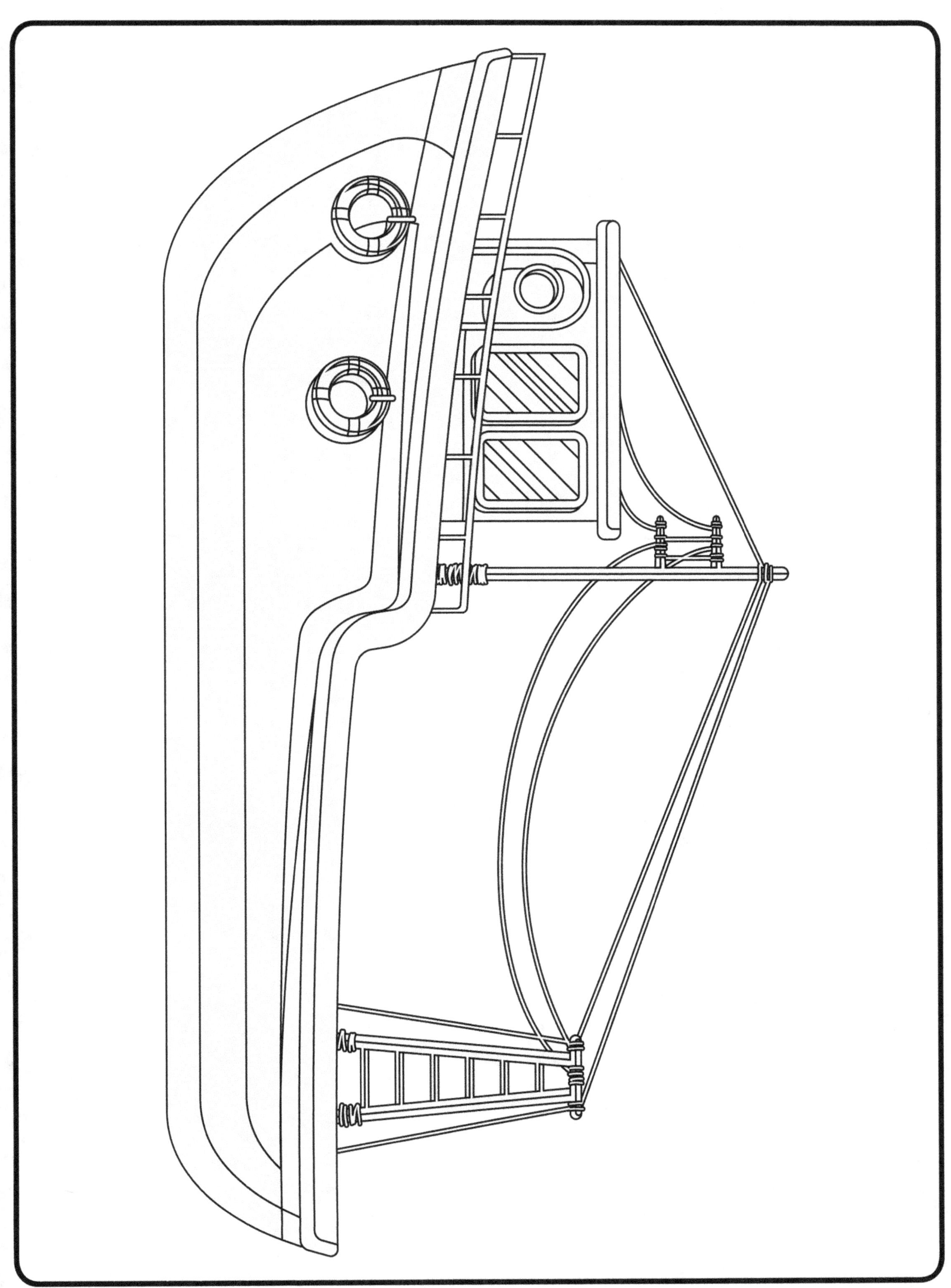

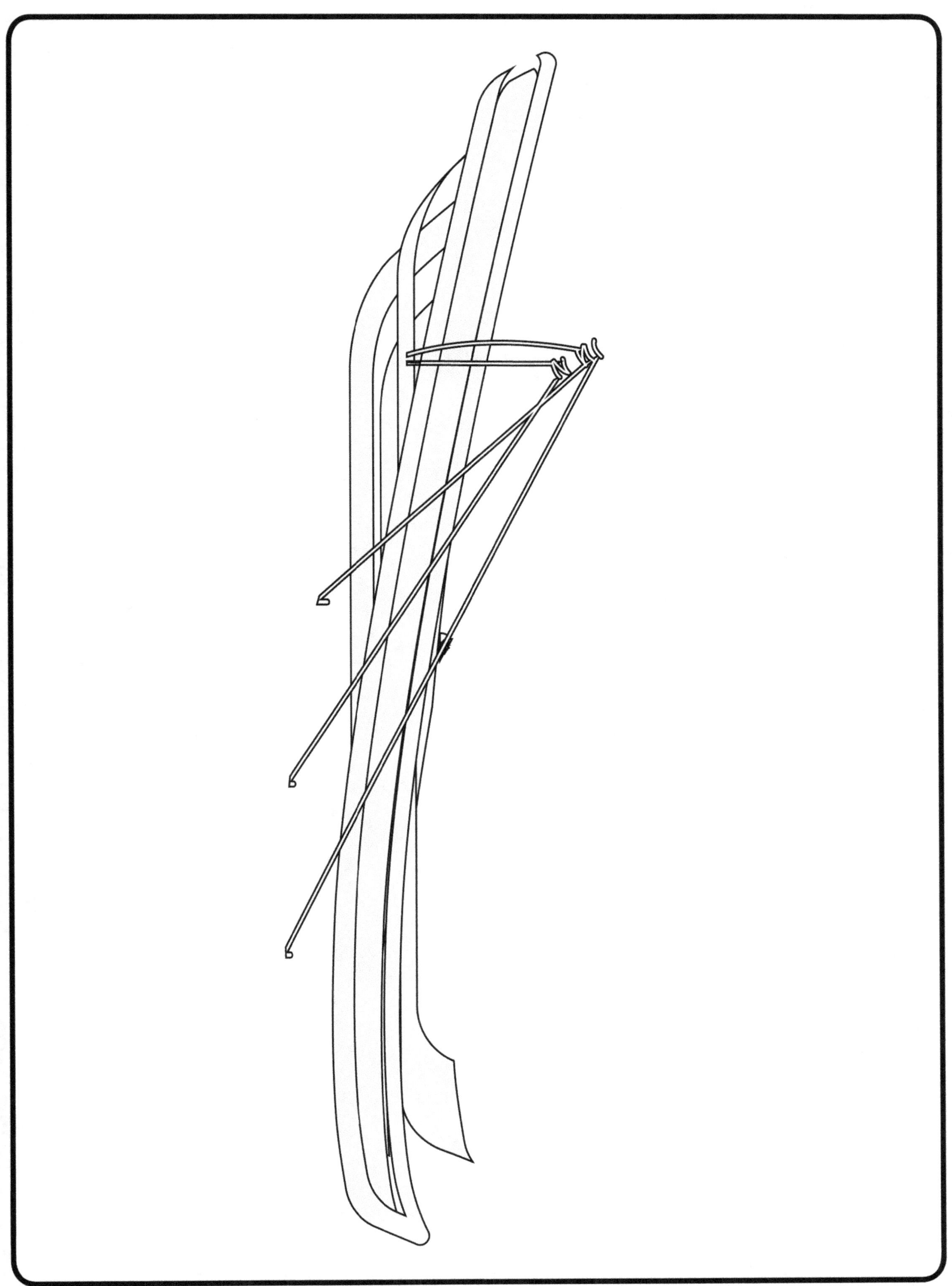

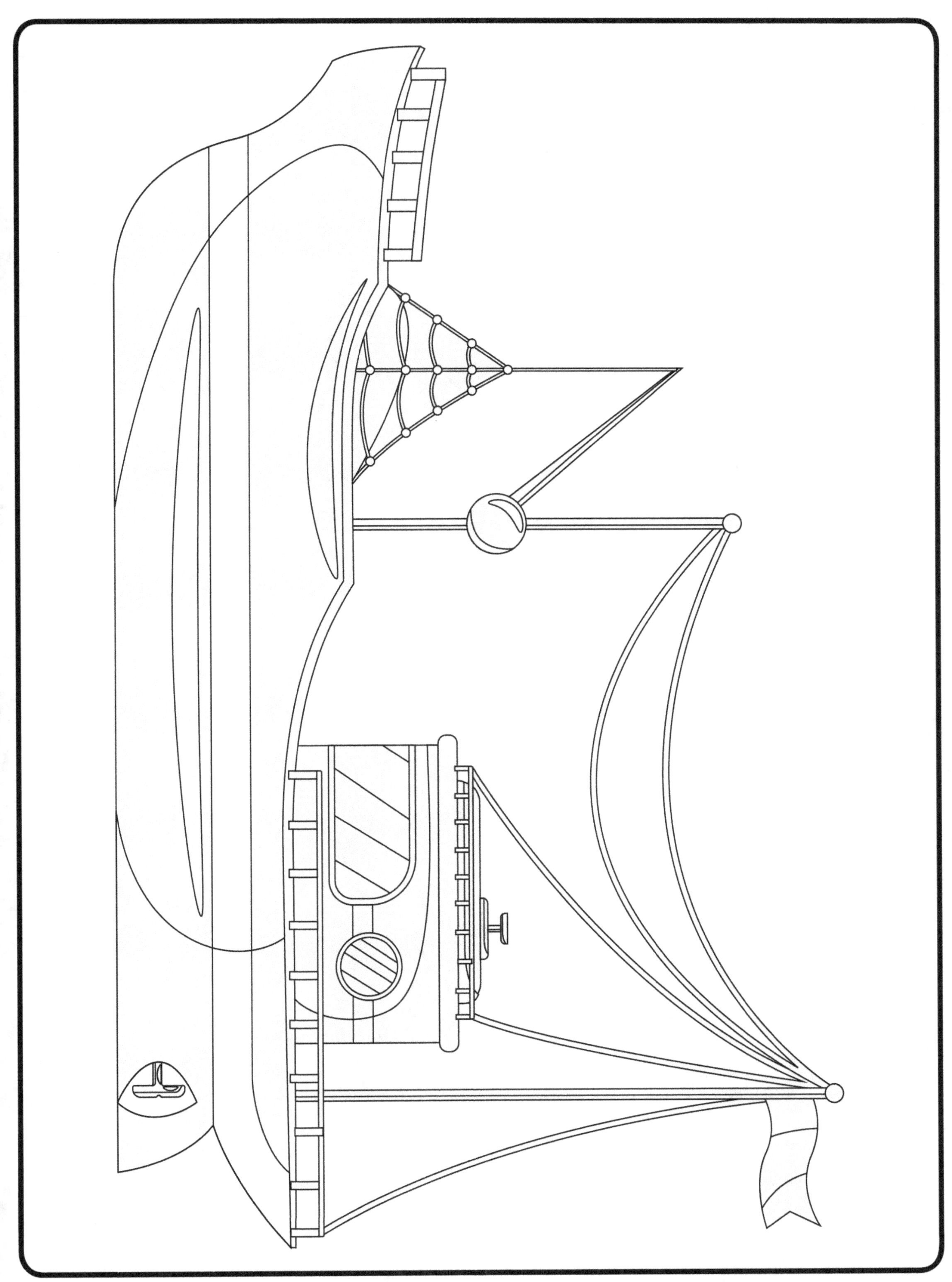

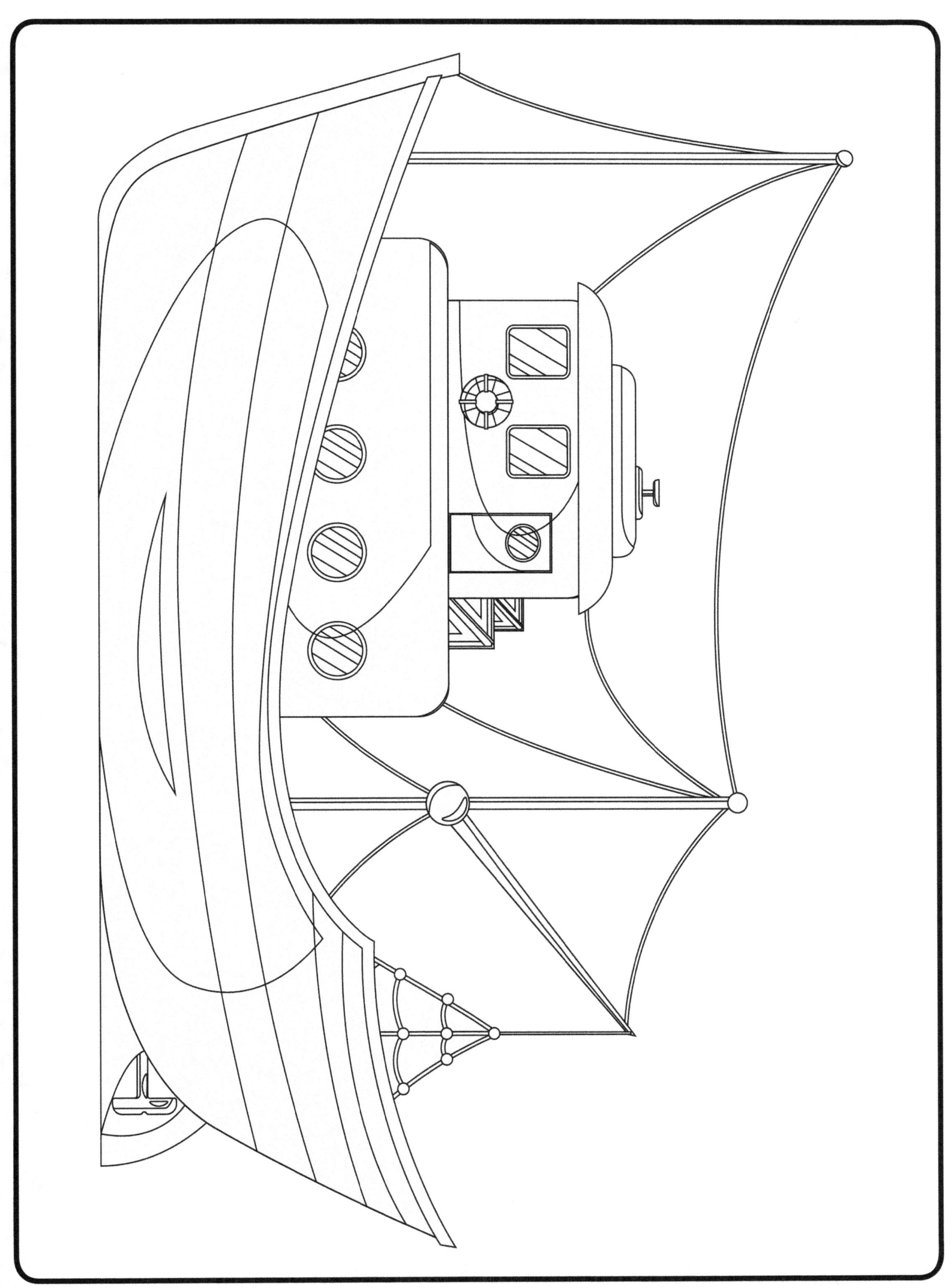

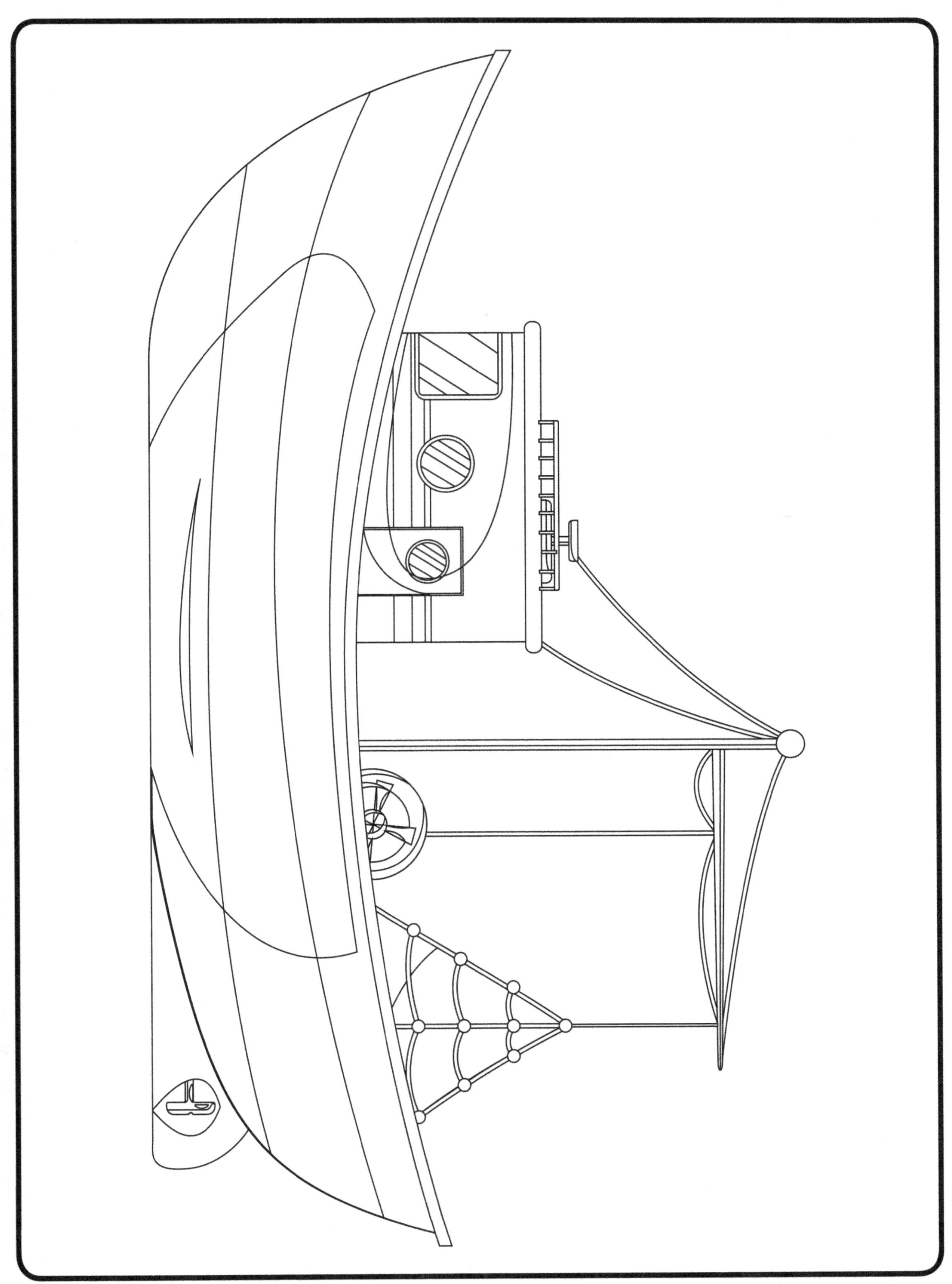

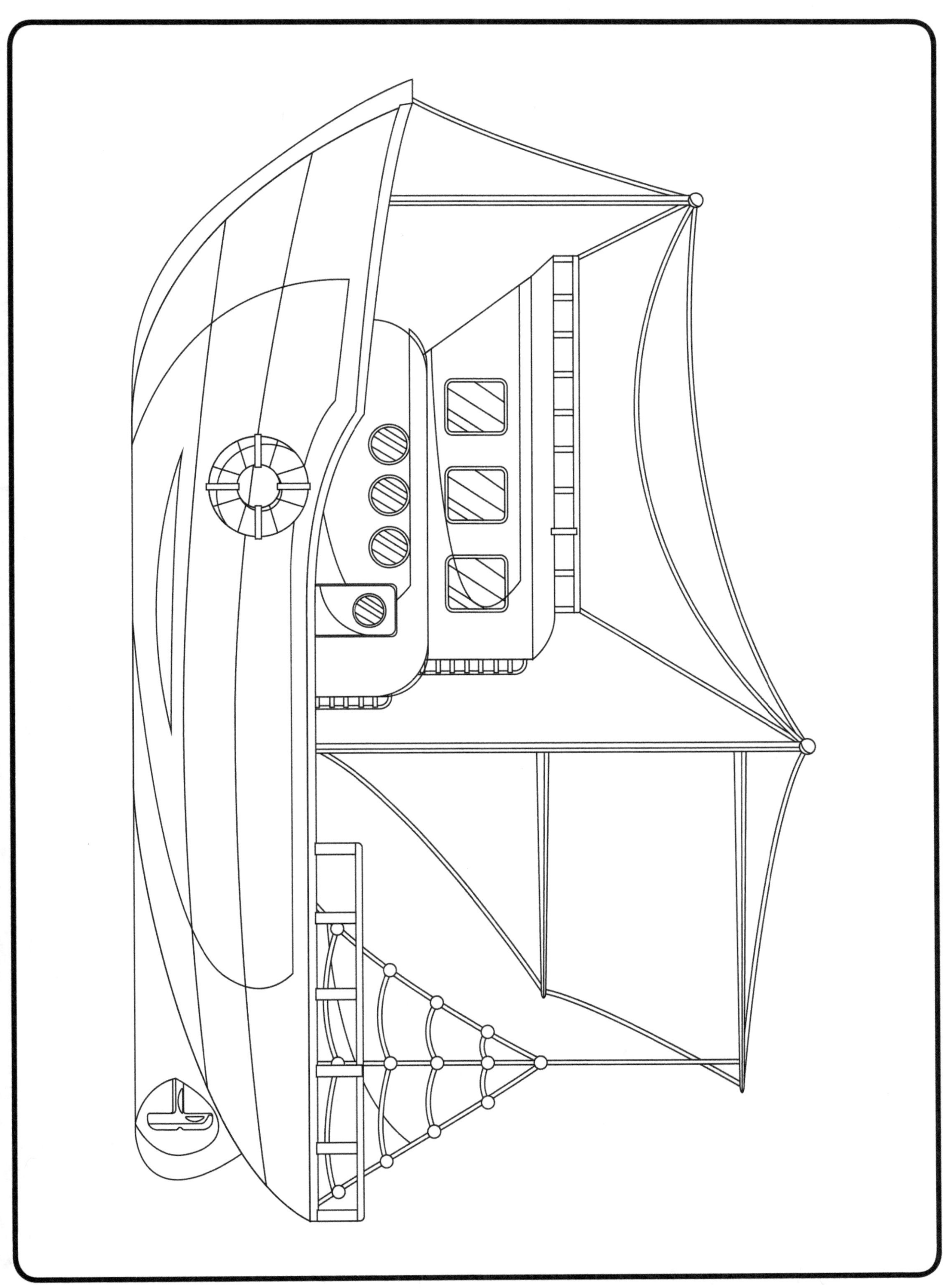

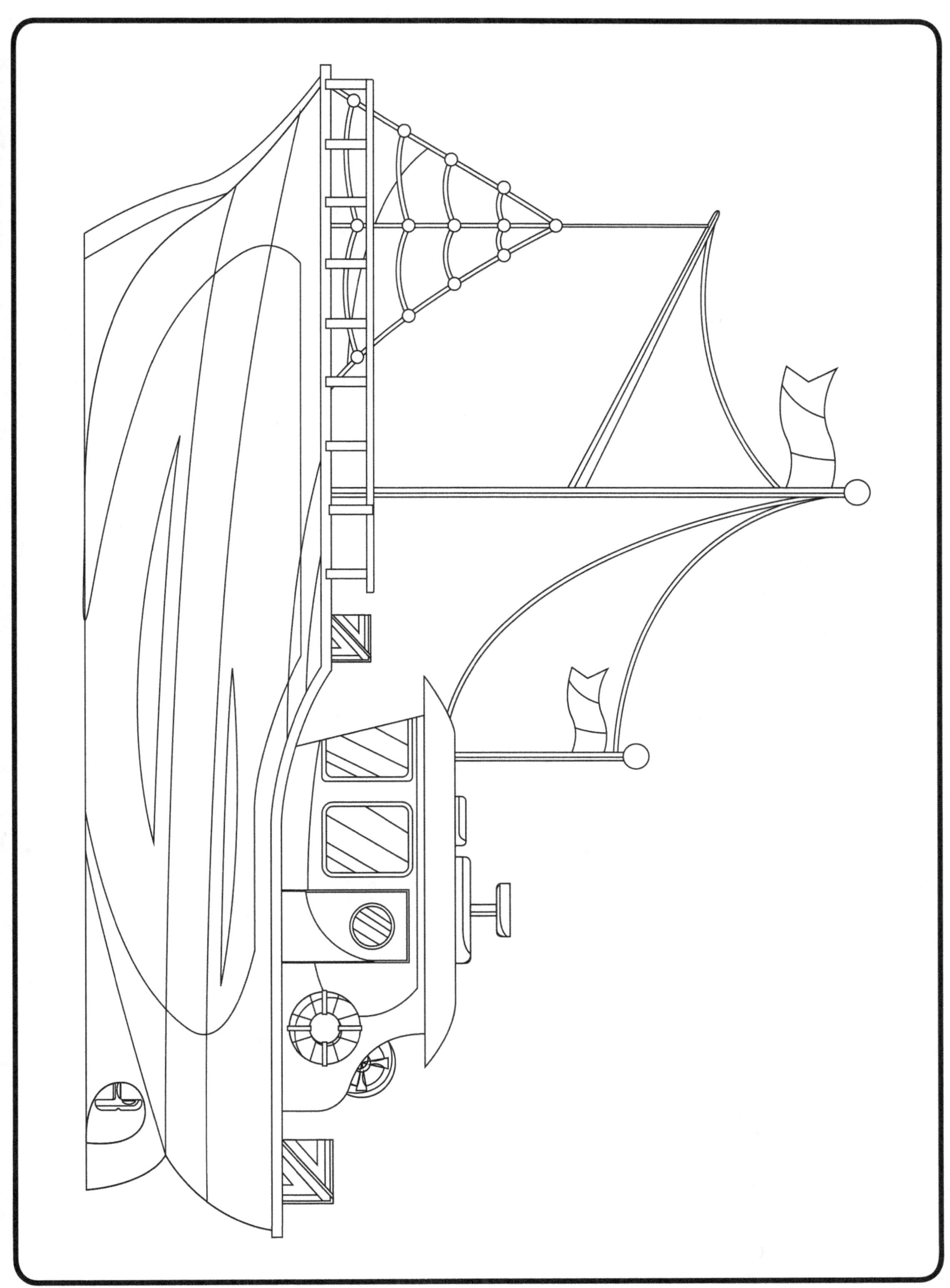

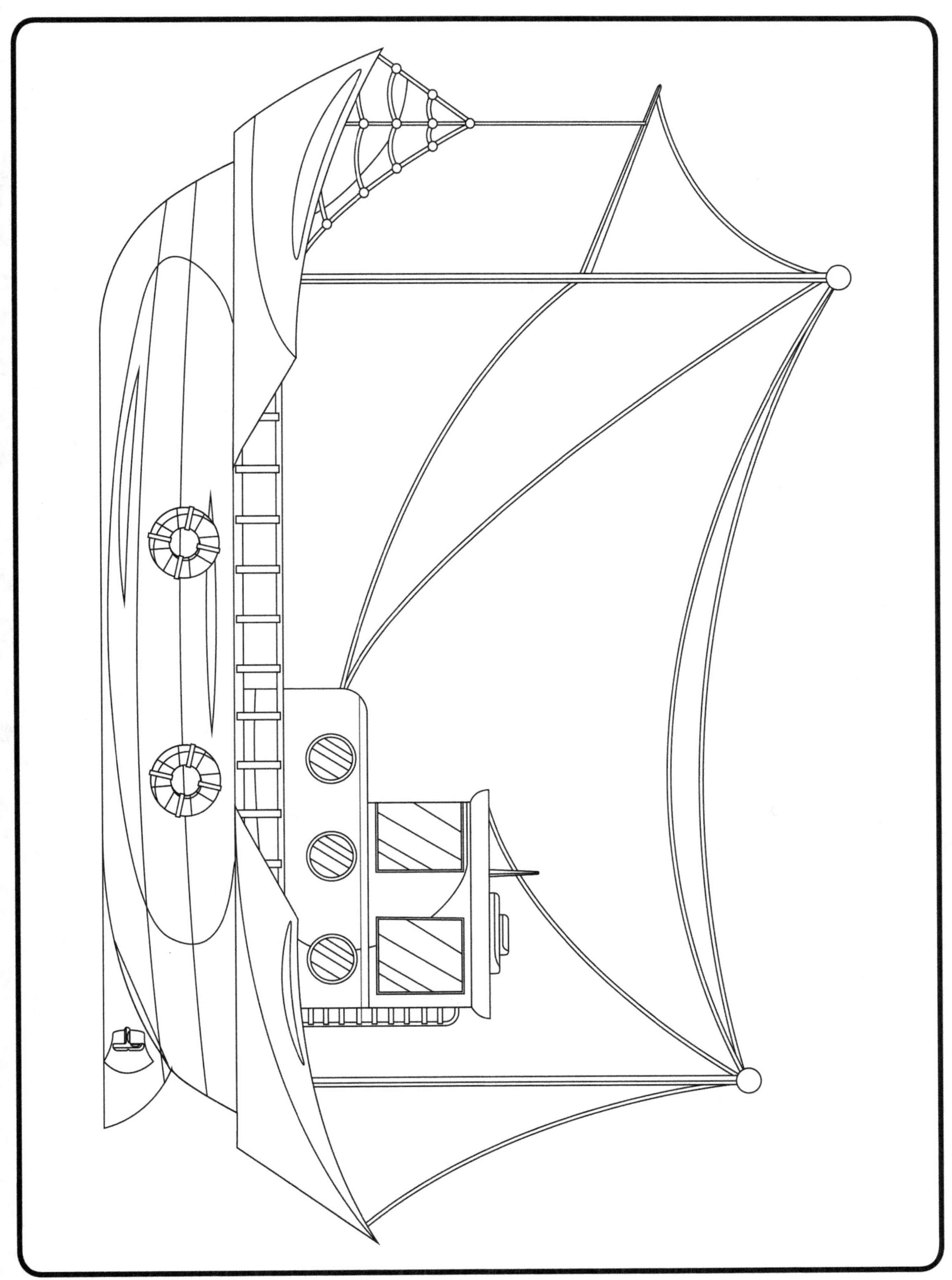

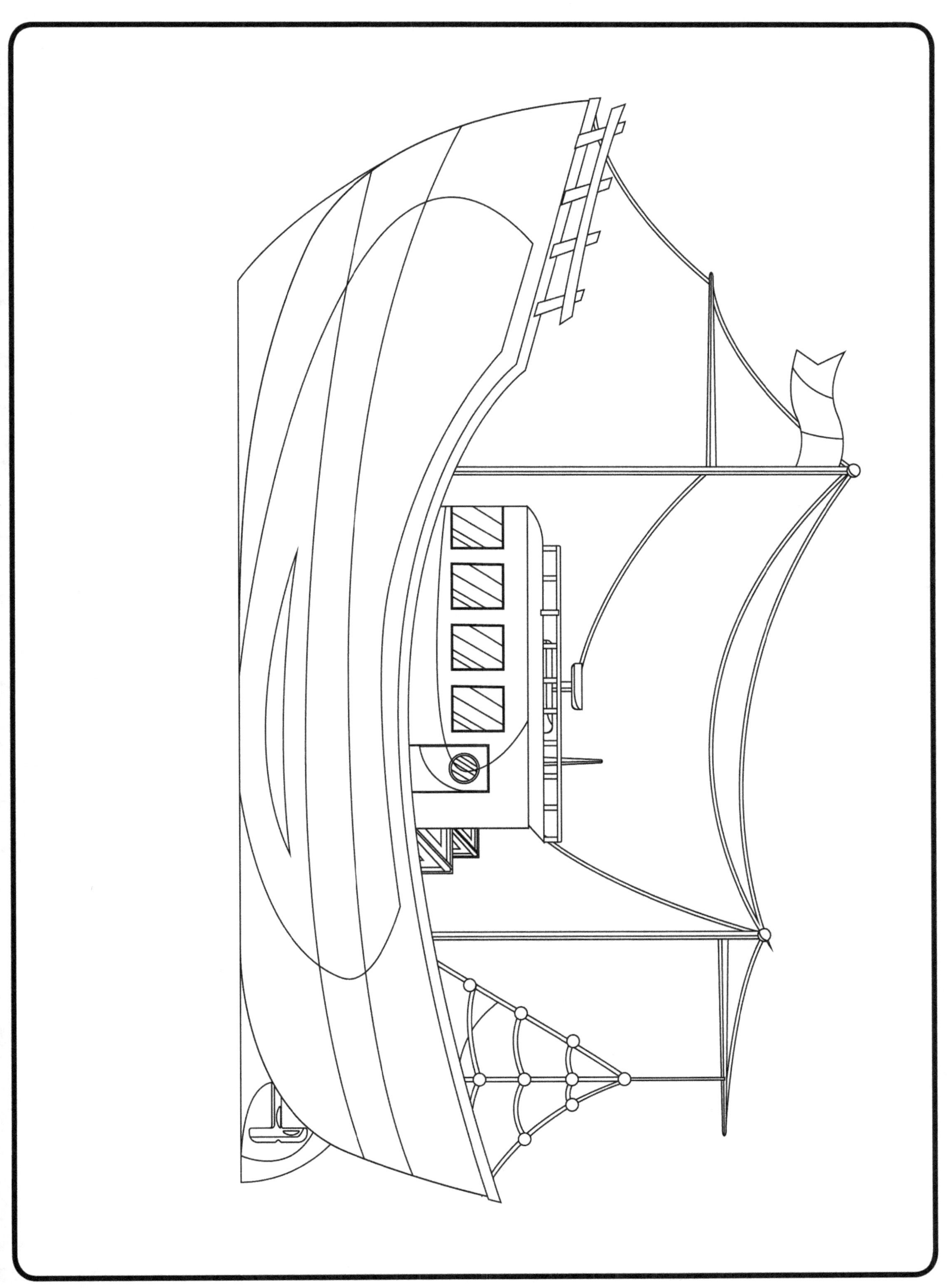

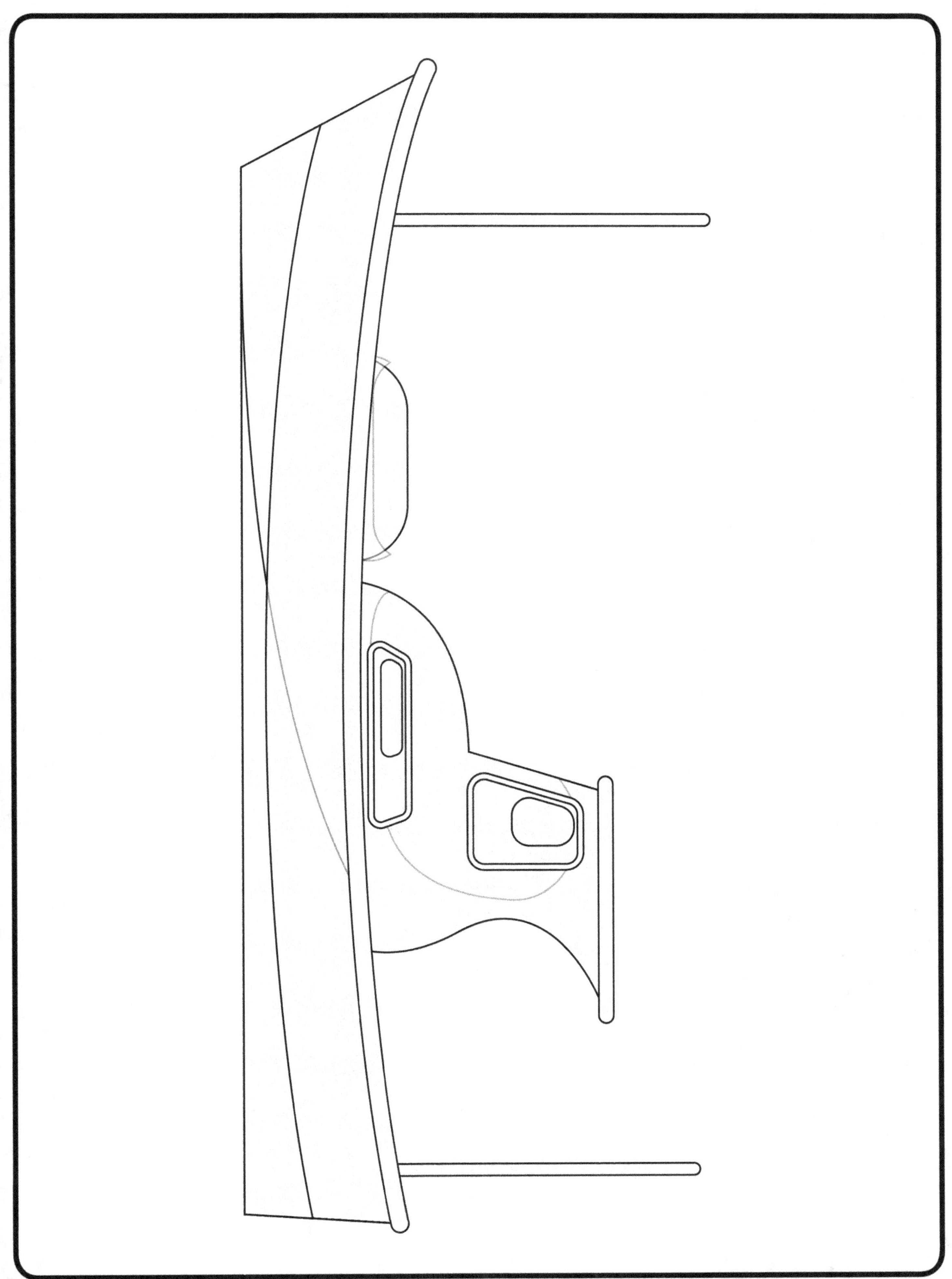

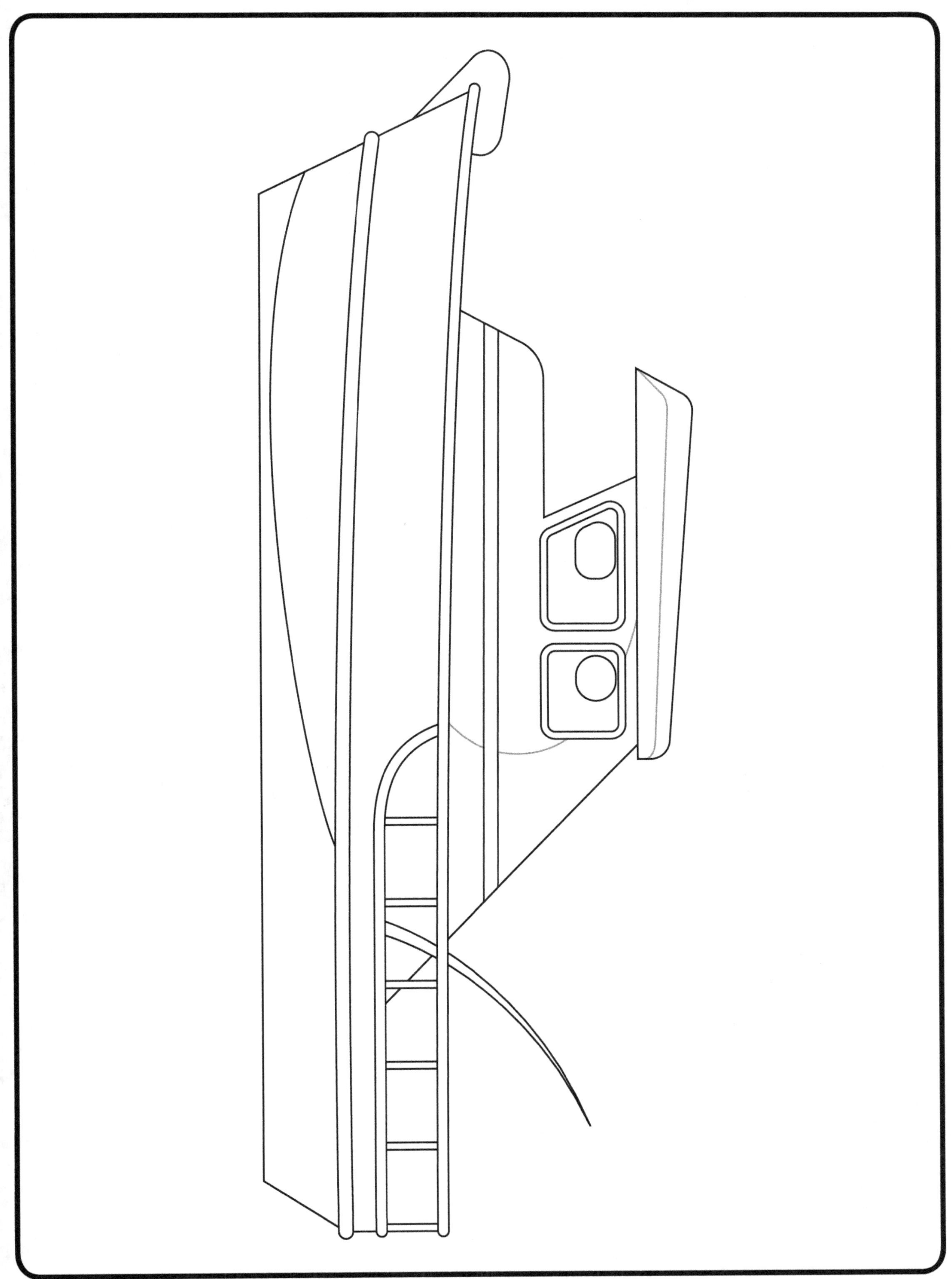

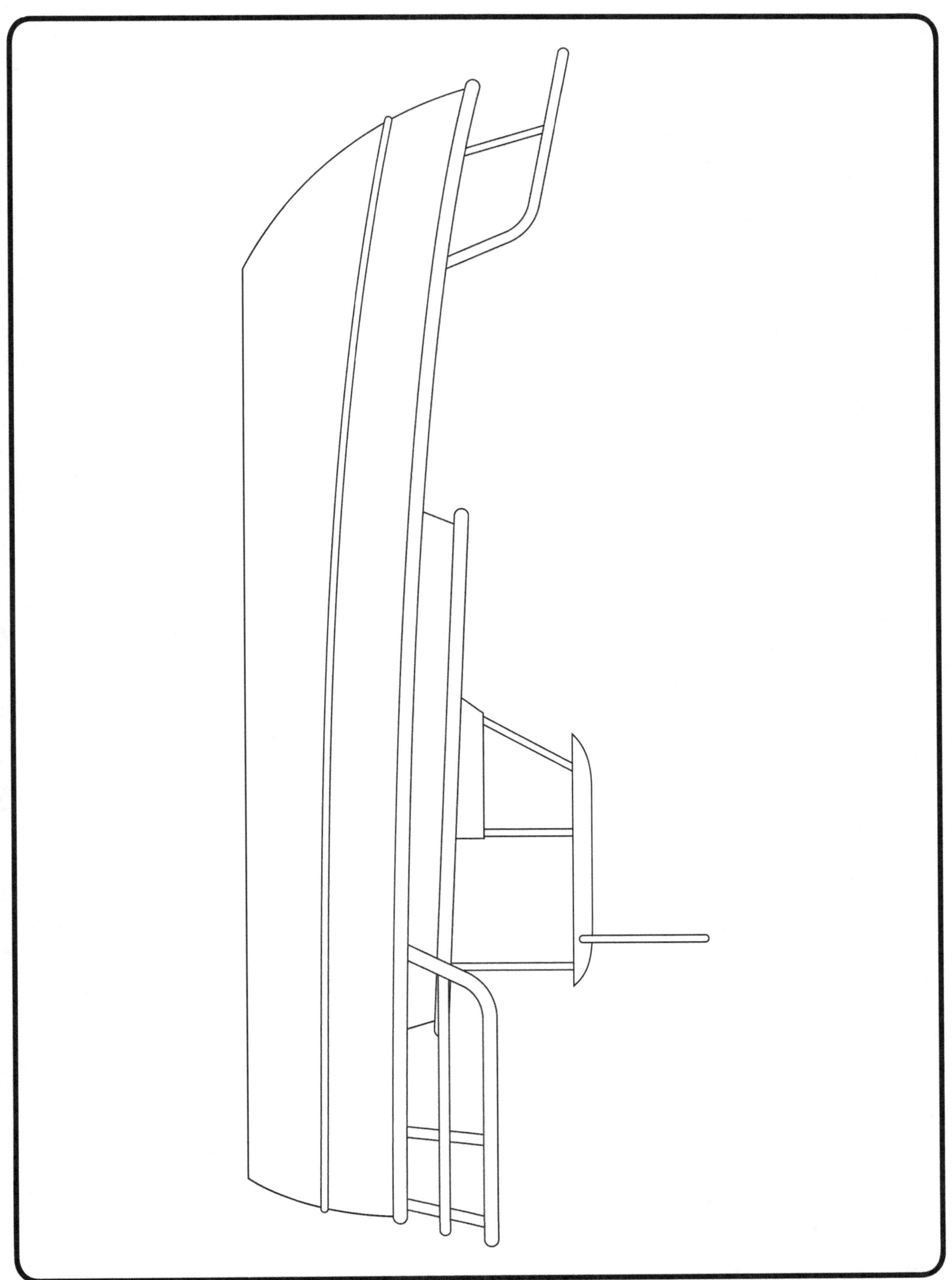